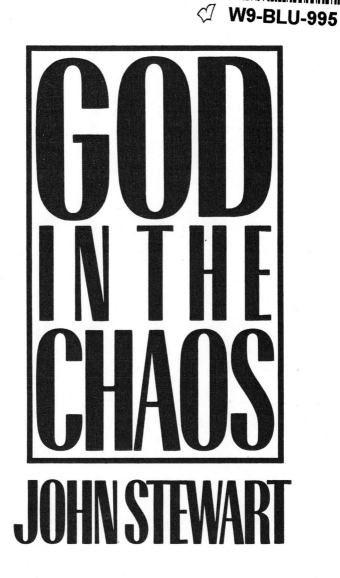

GOD IN THE CHAOS

JOHN STEWART

HARVEST HOUSE PUBLISHERS
Eugene, Oregon 97402

GOD IN THE CHAOS

Copyright © 1991 by John Stewart
Published by Harvest House Publishers
Eugene, Oregon 97402

Library of Congress Cataloging-in-Publication Data

Stewart, John, 1951-
    God in the chaos : living a dynamic Christian life in a Post-Christian
world / John Stewart.
    ISBN 0-89081-836-3
    1. Christianity—20th century.   2. Christian life—1960-
I. Title.
BR121.2.S75   1991
261—dc20   91-39157
                                                                CIP

To Jan, Jeff, and Jamie, for helping me through the chaos;

To my mother, Edie, who is to me what Monica was to St. Augustine;

To countless thousands of listeners whose encouragement and input helped give rise to this book;

To all who contributed directly or indirectly to make this book a reality, especially Eileen Mason, Bill Jensen, Rob Davis, and my brother Don.

Contents

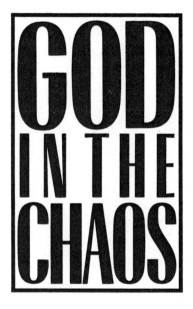

1

God in the Chaos

In the shadow of the twenty-first century, the pace and complexity of life have greatly accelerated. Rapid changes are occurring which affect everyone. Along with these changes have come confusion and chaos at every level of society. Externally, the recognition of our fragile environment has renewed fear that we are falling headlong into an ecological abyss. Internally, philosophers, sociologists, and theologians are concerned with the disintegration of the very fabric of our culture. The growing feeling that our world is on a collision course, with danger from within and from without, has brought about an urgent search for solutions. How can mankind survive? Can we regain meaning in our lives? Will the world ever make sense again?

In October 1989, tens of millions of Americans were focusing their attention on San Francisco, California—the scheduled site of the first game of baseball's World Series. What made this fall classic extraordinary was the fact that two Bay-area teams were competing: the Oakland A's and the San Francisco Giants. The game was set to begin at 5:30P.M., Pacific time. I was on the air doing my daily radio broadcast from southern California when, a few minutes after 5:00 P.M., the first reports came in about a major earthquake in the San Francisco Bay area. Despite all the hoopla, pageantry, and anticipation surrounding the World Series, less than 30 seconds of shaking changed all the plans and shifted all the attention. A bridge collapsed, an extensive section of an elevated freeway collapsed, buildings crumbled, and fires raged. Scores of people died, hundreds were injured. In under half a minute the lives of countless people were disrupted, some permanently. It had happened so fast, unexpectedly, and severely that people were left in a numbed state of shock. The horror of the "World Series earthquake" served as a stark reminder of how fragile our lives and best-laid plans really are and how quickly tranquility can turn to chaos.

In the past, answers to questions about life's purpose and meaning were readily available from a limited number of established worldviews. But just as the Ptolemaic solar system gave way to the Copernican, so also simple, traditional answers to life's questions have given way to modern, complex, and sophisticated responses. These contemporary solutions are of great concern to God-fearing people because the need for God has been virtually eliminated. The earthquake created by the gods of technology, self-sufficiency, and self-determination have replaced the need for dependence upon a transcendent Creator. Basic assumptions which formerly provided both personal and societal stability have been knocked off their foundations. What began as a faint quiver of change has grown into a massive upheaval, altering the structure of our culture as radically as an earthquake alters the landscape.

Cultural/Foundational Instability

What began as a shaking of the foundations of society has become a wholesale rejection of traditions. For example, well-established practices and beliefs concerning morality, marriage, family, and faith have been relegated to the dust of the past. The result has been an uncertainty similar to the unsettled feeling experienced during a major earthquake. During a large temblor, the most reliable, stable factor in life—the very ground beneath—can no longer be counted on for safe support. When the basic assumptions of life—such as the existence of God and a divine purpose for our lives—are not only challenged but criticized, rejected, and condemned, the emotional, psychological, and spiritual repercussions have the effect of a "life-quake."

The social, ethical, political, and spiritual crises which presently exist betray a deep-seated need for cultural stability. In an age of pluralism, the sheer number of competing attempts to make sense out of our age is mind-boggling and discouraging. Even if the number of proposed solutions to cultural upheaval were reduced to those involving "God," the diversity and contradiction would be enormous. For example, is the divine path to proper living found among shaved-headed devotees in saffron gowns? How about in Christian Science reading rooms? Perhaps in Moslem mosques?

Arguably, the most consistent factor in maintaining peace, cooperation, and brotherhood among all people has been the gospel of Jesus Christ. Unfortunately, among the most divisive, intolerant, and judgmental people have been followers of Jesus. Authentic Christianity has been replaced by traditions which deny the biblical teachings of love, forgiveness, and salvation. The Christian faith is either vaporized into a nebulous philosophy or frozen into a rigid, legalistic system of dos and don'ts. Those who have a balanced belief system often isolate themselves from those who could benefit from Christian examples. To make matters worse, it has become alarmingly common for believers to live in such a manner that they are indistinguishable from unbelievers. The world has become a fragmented place with people pulling different directions. Where is the power of the gospel to transform individuals and society? Where is the Christian influence in shaping society? Where is God in all the chaos and confusion?

Nineteenth-Century Methods
Applied to Twenty-First-Century Problems

Jesus said that His followers were "the light of the world" (Matthew 5:14). For this light to serve its purpose, Christians must occupy conspicuous places in society (Matthew 5:16). Dynamic, intelligent, and informed believers are the beacon which can guide culture past the rocky shoals which threaten to dash civilization to pieces. The "true light" (John 1:9) will outshine all the pretenders and help people out of the darkness, while making sense of the chaos.

Similarly, Jesus called His followers the "salt of the earth" (Matthew 5:13). Salt preserves as well as provides flavor. For society to endure the chaos and confusion of our age, Christians must fulfill their function of preserving. This happens by combating moral and spiritual decay through showing those in darkness a better way. Believers also represent the means to provide a divine flavor for society. But the distinct, penetrating taste and effect of salt is rendered useless when it is contaminated with foreign substances (Matthew 5:13). When the church is influenced by the world instead of vice versa, the corruption of both is accelerated.

Despite the willingness of the church to fulfill her role as salt and light in the world, the results are often insignificant, if not imperceptible. The simple truth is that the church at the end of the twentieth century is using nineteenth-century methods to reach people with twenty-first-century problems. The fact that Christianity continues to advance in some areas of the world is more a tribute to the power of God than to the success and obedience of His followers. The church has forgotten her activist roots and is trying to keep a finger in the dike when the entire dam needs to be rebuilt. For biblical order to come forth from societal chaos, contemporary methods of evangelism, discipleship, and community involvement for believers must be developed and applied. Innovation has to replace reliance upon comfortable, familiar, and outmoded methods of outreach and activism. It can no longer be business as usual if the church is going to be a major factor in charting a new course for civilization.

Traditionally, when the ground beneath begins to sink, many people turn to the solid Rock, Jesus Christ—the biblical Anchor for those caught in a sea of uncertainty. But something is amiss. The situation is similar to that in the well-known poem "Casey at Bat." The good people of Mudville put their trust in Casey, their home-run-hitting hero. Despite their confidence and cheers, when they needed him the most, Casey struck out, resulting in Mudville losing the game and their joy. When the complex problems of the 1990s are addressed by the church, the proposed answers and solutions ring hollow. There is no joy in the church for the traditional answers have struck out. Instead of a joyous confidence there is confusion, conflict, and chaos.

Christianity has been able to bring hope to the hopeless due to its life-changing message of love and forgiveness. But followers of Jesus have frequently been infected with over-belief and even credulity. Although not unique to Christianity, the denial of reality—including the reality of failure or mediocre results—has hindered the church from a realistic assessment of her effectiveness. Like the eternal optimist who, as he fell from a 100-story building, was heard to say while passing the fiftieth floor during his descent, "So far so good," the church has donned rose-colored glasses when viewing her impact on the world.

Denying the existence of a chaotic, confused world doesn't change anything. But recognizing the situation and responding with a well-reasoned, biblically based plan of attack offers hope. Instead of lamenting the problems of our day, why not view our cultural chaos as an unprecedented opportunity for reaching this generation with the stabilizing message of God's plan?

Communicating the Message

If the task of the church is to testify of God's saving power and love, the question remains as to how to most effectively communicate the timeless message of love and salvation. The apostle Paul said he had "become all things to all men" so that he might "by all means save some" (1 Corinthians 9:22). Adapting a message of hope, love, and forgiveness to the language of contemporary society is the challenge for believers.

Suppose a Christian wanted to take the gospel to unreached tribes of Africa or Asia. In order to have an impact, the person must be willing to learn the language and culture of the people he intends to reach. He then brings the good news to them in a way which takes into account their values, customs, and morals. The message is presented through means which are tailor-made for the intended audience.

For Christians in Western society, making an impact is no different. The language, values, and assumptions of society must be considered. Then once the "pulse" of the community or culture is found, the Christian message can be effectively communicated. The common denominator between the successful impact of Christianity upon Third World tribes and modern communities is *relevance*. An unchanging message is presented to changing systems of beliefs and values through proclamation that takes into account the special needs of the intended audience.

Relevance is the key to effectively reaching the world with the gospel of Christ. If the church has failed in any area, she has failed to be relevant. A message which is pertinent in resolving the inner conflict of people and which makes sense out of the chaos will be received with gladness. The church needs to spend more time listening to the problems of the world so that she can present an appropriate way out of the chaos which both individuals and society as a whole can understand.

Lest the essence of "relevance" be misunderstood, it must be emphasized that the problem of effectiveness does not rest with the Scriptures. "The word of God is living and active and sharper than any two-edged sword" (Hebrews 4:12). The Lord told Isaiah the prophet, "[My word] shall not return to Me empty" (Isaiah 55:11). The problem rests with believers who are unwilling, unprepared, or afraid to confront unbelief in enemy territory. In essence we have failed to be activists who pursue individual and societal change. Jesus said, "Go into all the world and preach the gospel to all creation" (Mark 16:16). He also taught in the parable of the sower that the sower "went out to sow" (Matthew 13:3) and that the field where the seed was sown "is the world" (Matthew 13:38). Presently, the church considers evangelism to be an altar call during a Sunday morning church service. Rather than taking the seed out to the world where it's needed, the church keeps the seed under lock and key. Once per week it's as if a sign were placed outside the church saying, "Gospel spoken here. Inquire within."

In the early 1970s a small church in southern California recognized the need to reach out to hippies, surfers, long-hairs, and others involved in the "love generation" counterculture. Rather than perpetuating an environment of wing tips, coats and ties, and organ-led hymns, the church created a come-as-you-are atmosphere which welcomed anybody. Although it was uncomfortable for an older generation to tolerate bare feet, casual clothing, and "street people," there were enough Christians praying for an evangelism explosion that they figured these ragtag youth were the answer to their prayers. Plus they figured that God knew what He was doing.

Contemporary music, some of it written the day it was performed, was heard at the nightly services. Street witnessing and beach evangelism took place during the day. It didn't take long for word to get out that things were happening at the little church on the Santa Ana/Costa Mesa border. The program of this church was relevant to the needs of the people who flocked to the service night after night. The willingness of that little church and its pastor, Chuck Smith, enabled Calvary Chapel to become world renowned for the number of conversions which took place, the massive water baptisms in the Pacific Ocean, and the contemporary Christian music which began a whole new musical style.

The "Jesus Movement" of the early 1970s had perhaps its most definitive expression in the ministry of Calvary Chapel. Church-growth analysts may have sophisticated explanations of why this particular church was at the hub of a nationwide movement. But the relevance of the Costa Mesa church in addressing the peculiar needs of southern California made it a prime example of what the "Jesus Movement" was all about: Jesus moving. It's a movement that began 2000 years ago and continues to this day. Wherever believers are willing to take the time and pay the price necessary for relevant ministries, Jesus will be moving. Hundreds of thousands of people know from experience the difference it makes when churches and ministries adjust their programs to the current needs of people. An example of the fruit of relevant ministry is the author's conversion and calling to the ministry, which occurred during the "Jesus Movement" in early 1970 at the (then) small church on the Santa Ana/Costa Mesa border in southern California.

Obstacles to Success

The good news that relevant, adaptive churches and ministries continue to successfully reach their communities is tempered by the reluctance of too many churches to make necessary adjustments. In fact there are built-in obstacles to success which are being promoted as the means to success. Some of the obstacles are a result of secular, bureaucratic thinking which hinders efforts to reach society. One glaring example is an attempt by the

Missionaries of Charity, the order of Mother Teresa, to renovate two older buildings in New York City for use as residences for the homeless. The nuns planned to bear all costs themselves and anticipated providing shelter, food, clothing, and job referrals for more than 60 men.

Obstacles emerged when city officials demanded that the nuns install an elevator for handicapped tenants. The nuns responded that they would rather carry disabled residents up the stairs than spend an additional $25,000 on an elevator. They asked for a waiver, which the building department was ready to grant. However, the head of the city's Office for People with Disabilities entered the picture. She said, "In India they carry people in off the street, but that's not acceptable in our society." New York City would not tolerate nuns carrying people up stairs. As a result of this intercession, the nuns from Mother Teresa's order scuttled the project.

The same type of inflexibility exhibited by the government in the case of the nuns is frequently shown by church hierarchy. Rather than subjecting our showplace church buildings to barefoot rogues, we not so subtly communicate our scorn for those who don't conform to some preconceived notion about what a churchgoer should look like. The obvious consequence is that a whole class of people, some of whom are or will be the shapers of future society, get the message that they don't qualify for what Christianity offers. The churches who practice such a "respect-of-persons" policy probably mean well. But their chosen means to success—that of protecting their church—ends up rejecting some of the very people who are often the most receptive to authentic Christianity. Their chosen means to success has become an obstacle to success.

Another example is that of a church in California which is known for its "church growth seminars." The focus of the seminars is the success story of the host church and how others can achieve similar success by implementing their methods of church growth.

The folly of this approach to church growth is first that it equates "church growth" with evangelism, discipleship, and cultural change. Of what eternal consequence is packing the pews with people who are untrained and unmotivated to actively infiltrate our culture with biblical solutions? Without a plan to reestablish the prominence of Christian values in society, church-packing tends to isolate the solution-bearers from the very culture they are called to reach. This merely adds to the chaos.

Second, this well-intentioned yet misguided emphasis on "church growth" fails to take into account the particular needs of each church's community. Not only do needs differ from state to state and city to city, but problems and solutions usually vary from neighborhood to neighborhood. Trying to establish principles of church growth based on the success of one church is like trying to learn principles of military conquest by reading the story of Joshua's conquest of Jericho. A military leader who tries to copy Joshua's strategy of marching around the city once per day for six days then seven times on the seventh day (not forgetting to blow the trumpets and shout!) would be laughed out of the army. Why? Because it's clear that God gave Joshua a plan of action specifically created for the conquering of Jericho. The plan was not intended to be used elsewhere. Why then do church growth seminars not realize that what works for one church most likely won't work for another because, like Jericho, each plan of action must be created for specific situations? Relevant, effective ministry is discovered through sensitivity, perception, listening to people express their needs, and through prayer.

Furthermore, well-meaning church growth programs are no substitute for actively confronting our culture with a Christian example and a message presented in a relevant fashion. The vitality of churches and ministries is directly related to the vitality of individual Christians. However, for the vitality of believers to be translated into effective, relevant Christian lives, churches and ministries must provide relevant ministry to both Christians and unbelievers.

If, in fact, relevant Christian lives are a by-product of relevant, effective churches and ministries, it's no wonder that Christians find their lives chaotic. A common complaint heard from believers and unbelievers alike is that church is boring and irrelevant. Add to these complaints the criticisms which say the church is full of hypocrites, full of snobbish cliques, and is only after money, and a pall is cast over the very notion of involvement with a congregation or ministry.

The bad news is that too frequently the church is guilty as charged. Enthusiastic new converts become disillusioned at the infighting and "backstage Christianity" from which they thought they had been saved. Added to this is the perceived irrelevance of church services, which causes even mature Christians to feel uneasy about inviting people to come to their own churches. First the "irrelevance of religion" keeps many people from Christ. Then the effective proclamation of the gospel often convinces these same people of the relevance of Christianity. Finally, the weakness of the church causes new believers to wonder whether they might have been right in the first place!

The good news is that churches and ministries can produce relevant Christian lives though effective, relevant ministry. The sometimes-uncomfortable, yet necessary changes which must occur in the programs of churches are the prerequisites to assisting believers in achieving the upward call of God. At the risk of alienating some people who thrive on comfort, status, and stability, Christianity must return to the powerful, life-changing theme of a Christ-centered relevance.

So What?

The opportunities for skepticism and cynicism abound in an age where agnosticism is in vogue. People who confidently stand and express their convictions are about as welcome as heat on a sunburn. Beliefs, conviction, and certainty add pain to our chaotic age of nihilism (i.e., belief in nothing). Since misery tends to love company, misery detests those who don't suffer from hopeless despair. Hence the Christian who has personally experienced hope is considered by those in chaos as not only the enemy but somehow even the cause of the problem.

Hostility toward the Christian gospel is not without parallel. During the Middle Ages the Jews, who had been relegated to their own communities (called ghettos) within the large cities of Europe, practiced their faith unobtrusively. The tenets of Judaism included strict dietary and sanitation laws. While the Jews enjoyed the benefits of their faith, including spiritual as well as physical well-being, non-Jewish communities were ravaged by plagues. Gentiles could have looked upon the virtual immunity of the Jews to the plagues as something positive. Had they done so, they might have themselves adopted biblical sanitation and dietary practices, resulting in the saving of countless lives. Instead, the non-Jews chose to *blame* the Jews for the plagues, intensifying the hatred and persecution already existing toward Jews. Similarly, non-Christians often choose to blame the chaos on the ones who have found a way out of the chaos.

Once churches and ministries properly serve as models for effective, relevant Christian lives, it becomes the task of individual believers to properly respond. A willingness to conform one's life to the biblical pattern, together with the desire to obey the commandments of God, will enable us to enjoy a faith that is genuinely relevant. Believers can thus maintain a balanced approach to life which will enable them to apply their faith in the fast-paced situations which arise in contemporary society. Whether the area of concern is family, marriage, career, or ministry, a Bible-based, Christ-centered life will help individuals make the adjustments to their lives necessary for personal fulfillment and having an impact upon others.

Jesus talked about abundant life (John 10:10). He was likely referring to a life which glorifies God through pressing on toward the goal of the upward call of God in Christ

Jesus (Philippians 3:14). The ability to make adjustments to the way we think, believe, and live during our earthly journey is the means by which our lives grow in relevance and effectiveness. In the wisdom of God, the Scriptures are the rudder by which believers are guided into fulfilling, divinely relevant lives. The combination of biblical direction, flexibility, and adjustment afford us the chance to experience abundant life amid the chaos.

One of the primary reasons for cultural chaos and Christian ineffectiveness in cutting through the societal disarray is the fact that our present age has become predominantly secular. For the church collectively and for individuals to make the adjustments necessary to effectively reach our society, the particular problems of the post-Christian era must be identified. Once the philosophical, ideological and cultural enemies are understood, then, and only then, will Christianity reassume its place as the guiding force of our culture. Updating methods of reaching the world and altering our lives to enjoy and testify of the modern relevance of a timeless message will enable the Christian faith to regain ground lost to secularism. Once we have laid hold of the divinely revealed plan for society and our own sense of purpose amid confusion we can actively and effectively help others find God in the chaos.

2

The Christian Response to Secularism

During the first three centuries of the Christian era the followers of Christ made tremendous headway in reaching their society with the gospel. Their progress came despite the fact that the prevailing worldview of their day was hostile to the Christian message. Rome dominated the Western world, having crushed all its military opponents and thereby assuming the right to establish cultural values and practices. These included belief in a pantheon of gods inherited from the Greeks, emperor worship, superstition, and every sort of sexual immorality imaginable. Christians knew that the pagan philosophy which Rome had imposed upon the Western world had to be confronted head-on. Challenging the dominant worldview was risky business since Rome considered dissenters to be subversives and pests—threats to the peace and security of the empire.

Despite the hardships Christians encountered as they swam against the tide of popular sentiment, they advanced Christianity to the point where it replaced paganism as the dominant belief and value system. The willingness of those early Christians to attack unbelief on its home field was the main reason for the rapid spread of Christianity. The long-term consequence of their labor was that for centuries Western civilization was shaped by Christian assumptions and by a pre-eminently biblical worldview.

Throughout the seventeenth century, the rules of society were still determined and defined by the dominant value system of the day: the Judeo-Christian ethic, based on biblical absolutes. If someone held to agnostic or atheistic values, that person still had to communicate by the language, terminology, and value structure of the Judeo-Christian majority in order to be understood. The seventeenth-century English author Thomas Hobbes in his work on politics called *Leviathan*, effectively uses Christian values and terminology in making his case about the unwieldy structure of politics. The uncritical reader would tend to conclude that Hobbes must have been a Christian, given his consistent use of Christian principles in his writings. In fact, Hobbes was an atheist. But Hobbes knew well that if he were to communicate his ideas successfully they had to be couched in the "acceptable" terminology and value system of the day, which happened to be Christian. The values of seventeenth- and eighteenth-century society were established by the effectiveness of the church in maintaining a dominance in the marketplace of ideas. Anyone wishing to be heard and understood had to play by Christian rules.

But in the eighteenth century the tide began to change, marking the beginning of what was first a modifying of the rules of the game, then eventually a total abandoning of the rule book. The Christian assumptions of previous times became suspect due to questions raised about the reliability of the Bible. If the biblical text was not the infallible basis of faith and practice as taught by the church and assumed by the masses, then society's values would have to be rethought to conform with new realities. Without fanfare or even detection, the shift from Christian values to secular humanism had begun.

Undermining the Bible and God

A leader in the undermining of the reliability of the Bible, and hence the societal departure from the Christian assumptions, was the Tubingen School in Germany. The head of this school, which engaged in literary analysis of the Gospels, was Ferdinand Christian Baur (1792-1860). Baur focused on the sources behind the Gospels, including questions of authorship and literary style. His conclusions, dealing with the area of biblical analysis called "higher criticism," called into question the authenticity of the Gospels. For example, Baur concluded, based on his subjective assumptions rather than on objective data, that John's Gospel was not written in the first century A.D. Instead, Baur concluded that someone claiming to be the beloved apostle wrote the account called John's Gospel in approximately A.D. 170.

The conclusions of Baur should have been suspect from the beginning, a case in point being his view that John's Gospel contains "later Christological developments." Baur meant that no one in the first century could have attributed the sayings and miracles found in John's Gospel to Jesus. He assumed that such were too advanced and sensational for eyewitnesses to have written. He concluded that the Gospels reflect traditions developed and added after the time of Christ and the apostles. Therefore Baur held that many, if not all, of the sayings in John's Gospel were never spoken and the miracles never performed. Despite the determination of Baur that the teachings and miracles of Jesus found in John's Gospel are too advanced to have come from the pen of a first-century A.D. eyewitness, most Christians chose to ignore his conclusions and continued to base faith and practice on the Scriptures. But the seeds of skepticism were beginning to take root as the church neglected its challenge to "contend earnestly for the faith which was once for all delivered to the saints" (Jude 3). With the discovery in 1933 of a manuscript fragment of John's Gospel dated A.D. 125 or earlier, Baur's theory crumbled. But the suspicions he raised 75 years earlier accelerated the decline of the dominance of Christianity in Western civilization.

With the attacks upon the Bible in the eighteenth century causing a reassessment and partial abandoning of Christian foundations, intellectuals began looking for a mechanism which would explain things without the need to resort to God. At least in part this pursuit was led by those who desired to be masters of their own fate rather than accept responsibility and accountability to a Supreme Being. This innate rebellion against the Almighty took a quantum leap in 1860 when a former divinity student supplied the world with a mechanism to explain life without reliance on God. The man's name was Charles Darwin, and his book *The Origin of Species* marked a new era in the secularizing of the world and the regress of the church. Building upon Baur's theories of the eighteenth century, not only could the Bible be abandoned but now God could be dismissed as unnecessary and irrelevant.

Such thinking gave rise to the proclamation of German philosopher Friedrich Nietzsche (1844-1900) that "God is dead." Nietzsche was not promoting atheism. Instead, he was making a diagnosis of the condition of eighteenth-century Western civilization. The shift away from God and absolute values was apparent to Nietzsche, and he was concerned with what would replace the moral vacuum left by the vanishing Judeo-Christian absolutes. Nietzsche projected a future man who would create his own values. Nietzsche called this future man *ubermensch*, the "superman," and envisioned this superman leading mankind into a golden age. The seeds of secularism had grown into a forest of new ideas, and the results would be devastating.

The movement to replace the Christian assumptions of the eighteenth century with secular humanist assumptions increased in the early twentieth century. Despite the anticipation of Nietzsche's *ubermensch*, the end result of man's climb up Darwin's evolutionary ladder was not quite what

Nietzsche had in mind. In abandoning the Judeo-Christian model for human behavior, the "civilization" which forsook God and the Bible contributed to one of the most destructive events in the history of mankind: World War I, the "war to end all wars." In spite of the monumental loss of life during World War I, a postwar optimism soon emerged with secularists even offering a creed to guide the new world they envisioned. The *Humanist Manifesto* was written in 1933 as a charter for this new secular age since the Bible and God were no longer relevant.

Just as in the eighteenth century when everything was "coming up Christian," after the first third of the twentieth century everything was "coming up secular." Unfortunately, the "hope that springs eternal" didn't foresee the nearly 55 million casualties from World War II. The atrocities of the war included savage butchery and mass extermination of millions of people at the direction of Adolph Hitler. The horror of the Holocaust stands as a graphic reminder of the capacity for evil in the human heart. The millions of murdered men, women, and children also illustrate the consequence of the church standing by passively when affirmative and aggressive condemnation is required. The Third Reich reveals both the fallacy of attempting to achieve "utopia" without Judeo-Christian moral absolutes and the failure of the church to make an impact during one of the twentieth century's most difficult hours. The body count of both combatants and civilians is the legacy of morality and human rights gone awry. With the Bible abandoned in the eighteenth century and the need for God abandoned in the nineteenth century, the sanctity of human life created in the image of God has been abandoned in the twentieth century. The death of man created in the image of God made way for the secular humanist man, viewed as the by-product of fortuitous evolution. Whatever significance and value life held in past eras subsides greatly in the brave new secular world.

Adjusting to a Secular Age

In order to regain ground lost in the past two centuries, the church must recognize that there has been a reversal of the dominance of the Christian worldview. Gone are the days in which Christian assumptions undergirded law, morality, and government. No longer must an atheist like Thomas Hobbes use Christian terminology in order to be understood. In fact, the tables have turned so greatly that the use of Christian terminology and Christian assumptions in our secular age will bring about confusion and perplexity. The rules of the game have changed. A modern secularist is likely to blink in amazement at Christian values in a way similar "to a cow staring at a new gate," as Luther said. There are different assumptions, different values, and different terminology—only now the secular approach is dominant.

For the church to make an impact, she must learn to communicate biblical truths by means of the dominant assumptions of the day. Although the basic message of Christ's love and forgiveness does not change, the delivery of the message has to be adapted to the secular mind-set. Unless the church wants to be relegated to an ineffective "society of the saved," the gap of understanding between the Christian gospel and secular assumptions must be bridged. This demands a recognition of the situation and willingness to meet secularists on their own turf. Just as in the encounter of Jesus with the woman at the well (John 4:5-42), the means of reaching people with the gospel should be modified to achieve the best result. Since Christians typically insist on using assumptions and terminology that have long been abandoned by secular society, is it any wonder that we are making little progress in redeeming our culture?

How Not to Respond to Secularism's Foothold

The worst possible ways to respond to the dominance of a secular worldview are 1) withdrawal from secular people and 2) conformity to secular values and practices.

The tendency to withdraw from society is a practice based for the most part on a misinterpretation and misapplication of 2 Corinthians 6:17: " 'Come out from their midst and be separate,' says the Lord. 'And do not touch what is unclean; and I will welcome you.' " The pattern has been to treat "unclean" as a reference to *unbelievers*, instead of to *ungodly practices*. This error has hastened the decline of Christian influence in society.

When persecution of Christians was rampant in the first three centuries of the Christian era, the church had the fortitude and conviction to stand and fight. Despite the unbiblical theology embraced by some who taught that martyrdom was a guarantee of eternal salvation, Christians didn't generally seek martyrdom. But neither did they hide from it. Once Christianity had endured the Roman boot of domination and persecution, the church grew lethargic and ushered in dark ages which tested the very fiber of the Christian faith—not as a result of external persecution—but rather from internal corruption and the diminished need to remain alert.

The Roman emperor Constantine's supposed conversion to Christianity in the fourth century A.D. ended the persecution of Christians but was also the cause of a type of "nominalism." As in many Western countries today (especially the United States), during the era of Constantine people thought themselves Christians because Rome had been "Christianized." Despite the biblical requirements of faith and practice which precede the right to bear the name "Christian," in the era of Constantine citizenship in the Roman Empire was considered sufficient to be considered a Christian.

Response to the watered-down religion of Constantine's era which passed for authentic Christianity didn't improve the situation. The "separation" mentality sprang to life. Since martyrdom was virtually nonexistent in the Western world after the time of Constantine, what does one do to be guaranteed a place in the kingdom? Seek separation...isolation...withdrawal from the nominal Christianity of the day to a haven for true believers. Hence, the monastic movement began. Rather than obeying the commission of Jesus to go into all the world and preach the gospel to every creature (Matthew 28:19), the trend was to retreat, with the anchorite monks (an order committed to withdrawing) leading the way.

Reversing the Trends of Separation and Conformity

There has consistently been a segment within Christianity which retreats during times of adversity and even during times of prosperity. The retreat can take the form of actual separation from society, as with the anchorites. But there are many who retreat into a Christian ghetto within society, sometimes retreating into esoteric discussions of the "inner life." For example, the seventeenth century saw the rise of a movement called "Pietism," which began with after-church discussions of the sermon and developed into a separatist movement in quest of a "deeper faith." The further the pietists retreated into their own spirituality, attempting to obtain the reward of perfection, the further they withdrew from any meaningful basis by which to reach non-Christians.

The pursuit of "something deeper," despite commendable intentions, tended to work against the command to reach individuals and society with the message of Jesus Christ. It is much the same in this modern era, where the dominance of secular values makes it difficult to make an impact through the Christian message. The time it takes to adjust methods of evangelism to the needs of a secular society, together with the awkward difficulty of confronting unbelievers, makes it easier and even desirable to remain on the sidelines and mingle only with those who are like-minded.

The price of authentic Christianity is just too high for many in a post-Christian era. So the church has adopted an attitude of isolation which effectively says, "If you can't beat them, separate from them." This type of polarization fosters suspicion on the part of both believer and unbeliever, and widens the gulf of understanding between the parties. If Christianity is to take the biblically mandated, correct path, it must renounce all forms of unbiblical separation—external and internal alike—and confront the world on its own ideological turf. And the good news is that the war is winnable.

The tendency toward spiritual and cultural isolation is endemic to conservative Christians, especially those considered "fundamentalist." But the response by liberal Christians to the dominant secular assumptions of the modern society is equally ineffective in turning society back to Christ. The liberal church, in its recognition of the inroads secular humanism has made in replacing the Christian worldview, takes the approach, "If you can't beat them, join them." The liberal therefore seeks to identify with secular society. The tactic is to show unbelievers that Christians really are not strange and ignorant (notwithstanding the "fundamentalist caricature"), but are really "with it." The problem lies in the fact that liberalism has become so adept in identifying with secularism that one cannot tell them apart. Like a chameleon which changes color to blend in with its surroundings, so the Christian liberal has so successfully melded with secular culture and ideology that nothing Christian is visible. A sincere, but biblically unsound effort to reach unbelievers has rendered a segment of Christianity virtually indistinguishable from the people it has attempted to reach. Is there any wonder that this type of approach has further muddied the waters and has fallen short of making a Christian impact on the secular society?

In presenting the extremes of separation and conformity which have hindered the success of the church in a secular age, there remains a biblically balanced approach which carries with it the realistic hope of making an impact on society. This mediating position takes the best from the separationists and the conformists but leaves behind the ineffective excesses which condemn both of them to failure.

The separationists act as if there were some virtue attached to the avoidance of unbelievers. Rather than encouraging avoidance of people, the Scripture is admonishing believers to avoid the sinful and ungodly practices that often accompany unbelief. Separation from sin, yes, but not separation from unbelievers. To deliberately associate with unbelievers is not to participate in nor condone any ungodly acts on their part. Jesus deliberately associated with sinners, yet never partook of their sin. The apostles did the same thing. Therefore, it is not only possible to maintain moral integrity while associating with unbelievers, it is *commanded* that Christians do so. The pharisaical attitude of superiority which is inherent in separationist practices must be abandoned if non-Christians are going to be reached in a biblical manner.

Maintaining a biblical morality is part of being distinct in a positive way (Titus 2:14). The failure to fulfill this admonition is the problem of the conformist. In sincerely wishing to reach his neighbors, the conformist has deliberately associated with unbelievers. So far, so good. But in most cases this tactic only brings about a resemblance to the world which further convinces the secularists that everything is fine and nothing needs to change. Whereas the Bible talks about transformation from the world's values by a renewed mind (Roman 12:2), the conformist adopts the world's values. Such an approach may win friends through a misguided tolerance, but lives are rarely (if ever) changed by believers attempting to be "hail fellow, well met."

The Scripture makes it clear that friendship with the world is hostility toward God: "Therefore whoever wishes to be a friend of the world makes himself an enemy of God" (James 4:4). It is the *contrast* between an unbeliever and a believer with strong, well-reasoned convictions that makes the believer distinct in a positive way.

The desire of conformists to win people's hearts and

minds to the truth of the Christian gospel through friendship and association is commendable. But only by maintaining a contrast between the transformed life of a believer and the values of the world will the non-Christian be aware of what God requires: a conscious decision to make Jesus Lord of one's life rather than a mere sentimental, moralistic embracing of traditional values or biblical ethics.

Learning to Balance, Not Juggle

The errors of isolation from the unbeliever and conformity with the world must give way to a biblically balanced method of infiltration: deliberately associating with non-Christians, maintaining a positive distinction in convictions, and intelligently communicating what Christianity is and why it should be believed. An old adage says, "The least convincing thing is the truth told unconvincingly." There is an abundance of non-Christians in a society dominated by secularism. In order for them to be convinced of the need to embrace the Person and work of Jesus Christ, the believer has to present an authentic Christian message using authentic biblical means, with a life that projects the reality of transformation. It's not an easy task, but the anticipated results make the endeavor well worth the effort.

The challenge to live transparently among unbelievers, allowing imperfections and failures to be seen, presents an authentic Christianity by means of a biblical method. There is something different about a Christian—not something innately better within the believer, but something that has been acted upon which has brought about positive changes. Not a perfectionism, but a recognition of God's forgiveness of failures and the ability to do better. Not a trouble-free life, but possession of a mechanism to understand and cope with adversity. Not a self-righteous superiority, but a humble acceptance of the grace of God. There is a great deal more likelihood of success in communicating the Christian faith if the believer comes across as a mere beggar attempting to tell other beggars where they can find bread.

3

The Battle for the Family

In the summer of 1989 the highest court in the state of New York—the court of appeals—decided a case which did away with the traditional definition of "family." The case centered around whether the homosexual partner of a deceased AIDS victim was "related" to the decedent by virtue of their sexual relationship. The surviving man, who had shared a rent-controlled New York apartment with the AIDS victim, was threatened with eviction upon his partner's death. Under the law, persons not related to the lawful tenant of a rent-controlled dwelling were subject to eviction upon the death of the legal tenant or abandonment of the dwelling. However, relatives of the lawful tenant were entitled to maintain occupancy of the dwelling at the rent-controlled price.

The New York Court of Appeals held that the term "family" "should not be rigidly restricted to those people who have formalized their relationship by obtaining, for instance, a marriage certificate or an adoption order." The court also said: "The intended protection against sudden eviction should not rest on fictitious legal distinctions or genetic history." In one fell swoop, one of the most prestigious state courts in the United States rendered the family a legal fiction, subject to redefinition by judicial decree. The court's same reasoning could be used to argue that a flophouse full of winos or even cell mates in a prison constitute a "family."

The Church and the Changing Family

Although the New York Court of Appeals has taken the lead in redefining "family" through judicial fiat, many states and local communities have seen similar challenges to the traditional family at the ballot box. For example, "domestic partnership" statutes have been proposed (and in some cases enacted without community approval) which provide unmarried cohabiting couples, both heterosexual and homosexual, with health and survivor benefits traditionally reserved for legally married couples. Without regard to the lack of legal status or moral considerations, cohabiting couples of the same sex are granted privileges which elevate them to a quasi-marital status.

It is not difficult to anticipate a time in the near future when cohabitation by persons of the same sex will be afforded the same legal status and recognition as traditional, heterosexual marriage. In fact, the practice of homosexuals participating in formal "marriage" ceremonies has been going on for years. It's only a matter of time before jurisdictions ratify such activity as constituting lawful marriage. And once the historic definitions of "family," "relative," and "marriage" are abandoned, it will be next to impossible to return to their traditional meanings.

From the earliest chapters of Genesis, marriage and the family have played prominent roles in God's program. From these basic units of human relations came the teaching of values, expressions of love, intimacy, security, and identity. Most wedding ceremonies employ a recitation of Genesis 2:24: "For this cause a man shall leave his father and his mother, and shall cleave to his wife; and they shall become one flesh."

Jesus recounted this scripture when asked about divorce, adding, "What therefore God has joined together, let no man separate" (Matthew 19:6).

The traditional definition of "family" is "persons related by blood, marriage, or adoption." Although some states elevate cohabitation between a man and a woman to the level of "common-law" marriage, most states require a marriage license for legal recognition of the relationship. But what of a couple which cohabits in a state that doesn't recognize common-law marriages? Does such a couple constitute a "family"? In the eyes of the law, no. Cohabiting in this situation affords no greater legal recognition than students living together in a college dormitory. Therefore, what is meant by "family" or "relative" has been well-defined in both history and modern law—that is, until recently.

Unfortunately, some religious traditions within Christendom have failed to protect the biblical design for marriage and the family. In fact, professing Christians have even supported contemporary society's attempts to redefine marriage and the family. For instance, in the fall of 1987 at the convention of the Episcopal Diocese of Massachusetts, a resolution was proposed for the development of a liturgy blessing homosexual couples. The delegates voted down the resolution 219 to 196. What is remarkable is the fact that the majority of the clerical delegation voted for the proposal: 114 in favor, 79 opposed. The lay members, who voted 82 in favor, 140 opposed, were the ones who defeated the resolution.

In May 1990 a lesbian couple was "married" at a United Methodist church in a church ceremony that included the exchange of rings and vows. The congregation disagreed with the policy of the United Methodist Church denomination on the issue of homosexuality and unanimously voted to bestow a "blessing of covenant or holy union" on "commitments that lesbian/gay couples wish to make." Without moral absolutes based on the Bible, legal distinctions (e.g., the comment by the New York Court of Appeals) and religious traditions change.

As perhaps never before in history, the church has an opportunity to promote the biblical model of marriage and the family. If the responsibility of the church to defend and proclaim God's design is abdicated, societal chaos could increase to unimaginable proportions. Without Christian families serving as models of the wisdom and benefit of functioning as God intends, little if anything is left which would hold back the brave new secular world from permanently altering the concept of marriage and family.

Parental Authority Under Siege

Besides the attempts already mentioned to redefine basic definitions of "marriage" and "family," the function of the biblical family is being usurped through often subtle, seemingly harmless events. An example is the parental authority issue. There is a growing trend in many countries whereby the government treats children as wards of the state. Beginning with the legitimate function of protecting children against abuse, governments have overstepped the time-honored barrier which grants parents the protection to teach and discipline children according to their own values. Under the guise of protecting children, Sweden, for instance, has outlawed corporal punishment as a means of parental discipline. Not only has the state begun drawing the line for parents, but it also criminally prosecutes those who would dare challenge its wisdom. The timeless teachings of the Proverbs which say that "he who spares the rod hates his son" (Proverbs 13:24) and "the rod and reproof give wisdom" (Proverbs 29:15) are dismissed as the barbaric practices of primitive societies.

Beyond the fact that parental authority is undermined and usurped through such practices as the criminalization of spanking, parents are also hamstrung by governmental efforts to keep them out of important decisions which concern their children. The abortion issue provides a clear example.

Many state legislatures have been influenced by groups which aggressively oppose laws calling for either parental notification, parental consent, or both before a minor could obtain an abortion. Notification and consent laws typically have a judicial bypass where the minor can be exempted from notification and/or consent requirements upon the showing of good cause.

California, a state which is very liberal in its protection of abortion on demand (due primarily to a California Supreme Court decision which interprets a "privacy" provision in the state constitution to include a woman's right to an abortion), was the scene of heated debate over the parental consent issue in 1987. Those who supported parental notification argued that, in other states with parental consent laws, teenage pregnancy rates had declined. Consequently, the number of births to teenagers and the number of abortions performed on teenagers had also declined.

The lesson from states with parental consent laws seemed to be that when laws encouraged parental involvement, pregnancy rates went down. Furthermore, it was pointed out that other problems among teenagers, such as drug abuse, poor achievement in school, and low self-esteem, were greatly reduced when the involvement of parents increased. Despite all the positive reasons for having a parental consent law, many groups were opposed, with many California legislators siding with the opponents. A parental consent bill was finally passed, only to have a superior court judge grant a request by the American Civil Liberties Union for a preliminary injunction against the law taking effect. The outcome of the parental consent law in California is presently in the hands of the California Supreme Court.

Although parental involvement has proven beneficial to teens experiencing difficulties, the absence of parental involvement places teens at risk. Without laws requiring parental notification before minors can have abortions, girls who are 13, 14, or even younger can make the decision to abort without the knowledge of their parents—a decision which could emotionally affect them the rest of their lives. Furthermore, if a young girl has medical complications from an abortion obtained without the knowledge of her parents, there is a greater likelihood that necessary medical treatment will be delayed.

Too many situations have occurred in which parents were unaware of their daughters obtaining confidential abortions, resulting in serious medical problems and even death. Such tragedies could have been prevented had the parents known about the abortion, which would have prepared them to be on the alert for possible medical complications. The hurt of finding out, after the fact, that one's daughter became pregnant and had an abortion pales in comparison with losing a daughter due to complications from abortion, especially when the death could have been prevented by the action of parents on the alert for signs of complications. Even the most apathetic Christian parents ought to be outraged that modern social engineers with the blessing of public schools have not only driven a wedge between parents and children but have also placed young girls at risk emotionally and physically.

Abstinence Unconstitutional

Attacking the family through reducing parental involvement with their own children has also surfaced in the contraceptive debate. Condoms are generally presented as the panacea for all problems related to sex, while sexual abstinence before marriage is usually downplayed or ignored. Parental efforts to have laws passed requiring the teaching of abstinence have been met with strong opposition. That anyone would oppose efforts to teach abstinence from sex until marriage is itself amazing. However, when the particular arguments against teaching abstinence are exposed, it is difficult to choose whether to laugh or cry. For example, in 1988 California parents convinced pro-family legislators to propose legislation requiring public schools to teach that abstinence until marriage was the only surefire way to avoid problems of venereal disease and pregnancy. The state senator who authored the abstinence bill was sent a letter containing the following:

> Dear Senator:
>
> The ACLU regrets to inform you of our opposition to [your bill] concerning sex education in public schools.
>
> It is our position that teaching that monogamous, heterosexual intercourse within marriage as a traditional American value is an unconstitutional establishment of a religious doctrine in public schools. There are various religions which hold contrary beliefs with respect to marriage and monogamy. We believe [your bill] violates the First Amendment.

The letter was signed by the legislative director and legislative advocate of the American Civil Liberties Union's California legislative office. Despite the efforts of the ACLU, the bill became law. Parents gained at least some assurance that heterosexual monogamy in marriage and sexual abstinence before marriage were being presented in a positive light in public schools.

Despite the California legislature passing a law requiring the teaching of sexual abstinence before marriage as the best practice, some schools took courses of action which sent mixed signals to teenagers. In May 1990 at Tamalpais High School in northern California, a teacher, the day before he died from AIDS, made his condition known to the school and his students. His presentation included a plea that students use condoms so as to avoid the tragedy he was experiencing, without regard to the question of whether condoms are sufficiently effective to prevent the spread of the AIDS virus. Tamalpais High School took affirmative action. The school decided to offer condoms to high school students without notifying their parents.

Under the program, the school nurse would provide free condoms to any interested students, but only after they participated in a 20-minute orientation session that included instructions on how to use a condom and information on sexual abstinence, venereal disease, and AIDS. The one-on-one sessions were to remain confidential.

Despite the apparent good intentions of condom give-away programs, the negative effect on the family is tremendous. Adolescents who have received religious and value-based instruction about sex from their parents can find their parents' teachings ignored or contradicted instead of reinforced. Ironically, in a state which has laws mandating the teaching of abstinence, a school policy making free condoms available has to cause teenagers to wonder whether adults actually believe that abstinence is a viable option.

Beyond the mixed signals about sexuality implied by the condom program, and beyond the likelihood that a 20-minute orientation system can scuttle ten years of parental advice, the worst tragedy of this condom debacle is the clear message that "parents don't count." To have public schools teach things contrary to the values of parents is not an uncommon occurrence these days. But when the subject is one as important as sex, and the school is providing the means by which teenagers can more confidently engage in sexual activity, to leave parents out of the discussion is a travesty. The authority of the school thus replaces the authority and responsibilities of the parents without their consent and without their even knowing what is being said or done which might affect their children.

The Resurrection of the Family

Borrowing from Mark Twain, who once quipped that reports of his death "had been greatly exaggerated," the reports of the death of the family have been greatly exaggerated. While the Ozzie-and-Harriet-style family may no longer be the norm, the family unit continues to be the bedrock of civilization. Despite the numerous factors which have threatened the demise of the family, including divorce, demands of the work force, and the lack of sufficient models of healthy families, the family continues to endure. How can we guarantee that this fundamental unit in society maintains its proper place in providing the nurture, love, and security God intended?

The Bible makes an inseparable link between the role of individuals and the health of families. Titus 2:1-8 serves as a leading passage which presents the biblical pattern for both personal and family health and well-being. Whether male or female, young or mature, each person is challenged to play his or her proper part within the family. The Scripture says that when we live according to these biblical principles, it also serves as an example to unbelievers.

Too few Christians recognize what an important part the family plays in the battle for our culture. Yet we can all join the battle by committing ourselves to doing our best to contribute to the well-being of our families. Paul's admonition to the Philippians seems tailor-made for this point:

> Do nothing from selfishness or empty conceit, but with humility of mind let each of you regard one another as more important than himself; do not merely look out for your own personal interests, but also for the interests of others (Philippians 2:3,4).

Standing Up for the Family

If Christianity is going to win the battle for the hearts and minds of our culture, it must first win the battle at home. Families are under attack on many fronts, including attacks on individuals which have the effect of disrupting the family, and attacks on the very definition and concept of "family." Since family health is no greater than the health of individuals who make up the family, it is vital that individuals practice their roles in accordance with biblical patterns. Likewise, everyone should be aware of the subtle attempts to redefine "family" and stand against this trend through the outspoken proclamation of God's design for the family and through being an example of how God intends families to function.

For those individuals and families which have become conformed to the worldly example of fragmentation, selfishness, and lack of direction, the Scriptures provide the means for healing. Taking the time to allow God's plan to transform through the renewing of one's mind will pay both temporal and eternal dividends. There are both the time and means available to protect and promote the family as God intended, even in a secular age. It is up to those who believe in biblical values to rise to the challenge, winning hearts and homes in the battle for the family.

4

The Turmoil over Ethics and Morality

How should morality be determined? Why should *I* be able to define right and wrong? What gives *you* the right to determine morality? Everyone has some form of morals. There is honor even among thieves. The question then is, Who's ethics do we choose? Which morals, if any, ought to be embraced by individuals and society? Why should there be any preset standards of right and wrong? Is it not best to maintain flexibility rather than adhere to rigid, anachronistic ideals?

Austrian philosopher Ludwig Wittgenstein presented a concept that was considered axiomatic until the twentieth century: "The sense of the world must lie outside the world. . . . Ethics is transcendental." The point of Wittgenstein's remarks is that our cultural and personal values are limited by our human predicament and finite experiences. Therefore, we must look beyond ourselves for values upon which society can be regulated. Otherwise, society would be governed by constantly changing laws, which have a way of degenerating to *argumentum ad baculum* ("might makes right").

Without absolute values undergirding society and the individual, we become subject to a moral relativity. The result of such a moral vacuum is that strong-arm tactics, expediency, and situational ethics replace existing standards of right and wrong. An example occurred during the "Big Three" meeting at Yalta toward the end of World War II. Winston Churchill mentioned a course of action suggested by the pope, which the pontiff felt would be morally proper. Joseph Stalin rejected the pope's suggestion by asking, "And how many divisions does the pope have?"

If enough people believe or practice a certain way, does that belief or practice become "right"? The *ad populum* argument that "50 million Frenchmen can't be wrong" is applied to almost every area of human behavior today. At first this "bandwagon" approach to ethics serves to destigmatize various practices. For example, the commonly presented argument which seeks to legitimize homosexuality is that "ten percent of the population is homosexual." Suppose for the sake of argument that the 10 percent figure is correct. Where is the logical connection between the number of people engaging in a practice and its morality? The inference is that if enough people act a certain way, the action at the least should bear no stigma and at the most should be considered "right." Unfortunately, the fallacy of using this approach to determine morality or acceptable behavior can be shown by substituting words such as "murderer" or "pedophile" for "homosexual." It is difficult to conceive of a healthy mind defending murder and pedophilia based on the number of practitioners.

The Lessons of the Third Reich and Nuremberg

In 1933, it was officially declared in Germany that the final authority regarding state and legal matters was the Nazi party. No other political party could be formed, and the fuhrer, Adolph Hitler, made all the laws. One might imagine that such a situation in theory might be workable. In the case of the Third Reich, the testimony of history proves otherwise.

The relative morals of Hitler included his notion of the superiority of the Aryan race. In isolation this view could be written off as mere racial paranoia. Unfortunately, there are consequences attached to such beliefs. In the case of Hitler, his conclusion was that the Jewish people were the greatest obstacle to the security of Germany and to the development of the Aryan *ubermensch* ("supermen") predicted by the atheistic German philosopher Nietzsche. As a result, the Jews had to be removed. But the ethics of Hitler went beyond deportation. His "ultimate solution" called for extermination of all Jews: men, women, and children. The millions of Jews who perished during the Holocaust serve as a legacy of moral relativity.

Once the Nazis had been defeated, the atrocities of Dachau, Buchenwald, Auschwitz, and other concentration camps came to light. As the world became aware of the unspeakable acts, cries for justice came from everywhere. For the surviving leaders of the Nazi regime, what standard of judgment would be used to try these alleged "war criminals"? The Allied victors of World War II established a criminal tribunal at Nuremberg, Germany, to prosecute Nazi leaders. A charter of the tribunal was drawn by the victors, which set forth the standards by which the accused would be judged.

Some Nazi defendants complained that they had simply carried out orders from superiors. Others defended their actions by saying that they had acted consistently with their country's own legal system and national interests. How, they asked, could they be properly condemned for deviating from the value system of their captors—a value system alien to Nazi Germany?

The issues raised by the Nuremberg defendants raises again the questions of "Whose standard?" and "Whose morality?" As contemptuous as the Nazi actions were, the Nazis were accurate in their complaint that they were being tried under *ex post facto* laws—a situation prohibited by the United States Constitution (Article I, Section 9). How could these defendants be properly accused of crimes which didn't exist at the time they allegedly occurred and of charges which were imposed by their conquerors, who embraced a foreign value system? What made it "right" for the Allies to judge the propriety of the wartime actions and policies of the German military? What gave the victors the right to determine right and wrong, other than the fact that they had won the war?

The Transcendent Law Versus the Natural Law

Despite the objections to the proceedings at Nuremberg lodged by the Nazi defendants, the prosecution prevailed. The chief counsel for the United States at Nuremberg, Robert H. Jackson, realized the weakness of relying upon the laws of particular societies in the Nuremberg trials. Instead, he appealed to permanent values which transcend the laws and practices of individual nations. In essence, Jackson relied upon the axiom of Wittgenstein that "ethics is transcendental." Neither the laws of the United States, nor Germany, nor any other country could have properly been used to convict the accused at Nuremberg. Hence, Jackson presented the prosecution's reliance on a "higher law" :

> As an International Military Tribunal, [the Tribunal] rises above the provincial and transient and seeks guidance not only from International law but also from the basic principles of jurisprudence which are assumptions of civilization.

One might argue that an appeal to "assumptions of civilization" is a question-begging return to mere human laws. How can civilization create "higher law"? Logically, it can't. Adherents to the natural law theory hold that absolute moral and legal standards are ingrained in the human situation and can be discovered as the common elements in moral laws and legislation of all cultures. These standards were regarded as proof of God's hand in the affairs of men.

The subjectivity and imprecision of relying upon natural law is evident. Wittgenstein's statement that "the sense of the world must lie outside the world" does not complement natural law, which relies on an intuitive, collective standard of ethics. How does one explain cannibal ethics or Watergate ethics, much less Nazi ethics? Are these not "assumptions of civilizations," too?

Instead of the vagueness of natural law, a higher law can be clearly seen in the biblical law of God. Scripture affirms the existence of moral absolutes based upon the existence of a moral Lawgiver. Whether over a period of two weeks, two centuries, or two millennia, there is no fluctuation in the fundamental values revealed by God. The assumptions of natural law pale in comparison to the objective, definitive revelations of God's higher law. The higher law, in its simplest expression, is embodied in the Ten Commandments (Exodus 20:1-17). It is more fully developed in numerous biblical principles, and finds its clearest expression in the life and teachings of Jesus Christ: "God, after He spoke long ago to the fathers in the prophets in many portions and in many ways, in these last days has spoken to us in His Son" (Hebrews 1:1,2).

The Benefits of Biblically Based Higher Law

There are three essential benefits connected to the understanding and use of biblical higher law.

1. Higher law constitutes an absolute standard of justice, whereby the ethics, laws, and deeds of men and society can be judged.

In hearing secularists discussing contemporary social problems, one wonders how these people can become so indignant about certain perceived "wrongs" while ignoring other questionable practices. Take the case of discrimination. Racial discrimination is commonly placed at the top of the hierarchy of cultural sins. Why? What makes racial discrimination more invidious than gender or age discrimination? None of these groups has any choice in the factor that is the basis for discrimination. Why is any discrimination considered morally repugnant, and why are all persons entitled to equal protection under the law?

If moral relativity occupied the field of law and ethics, the main objection to racial discrimination would be that it denies equal protection based on a factor beyond the control of the person. But what makes this "wrong"? Consensus? Experience? The Bible says that "He made from one, every nation of mankind to live on all the face of the earth" (Acts 17:26).

In the 1857 United States Supreme Court case of *Dred Scott v. Sanford*, black slaves were not considered "persons" entitled to protection under law. The Court decided that, under the Constitution, Scott, a black slave, was his master's property and was not a citizen of the United States. The Court also declared that the Missouri Compromise, which prohibited slavery in certain areas, unconstitutionally deprived people of property—their slaves! The Thirteenth, Fourteenth, and Fifteenth Amendments to the Constitution, adopted in 1865, 1867, and 1870, respectively, overrode the *Dred Scott* decision, changing the way the law treated blacks and other races.

Since ratification by a two-thirds majority of Congress and three-fourths of the legislatures of the states is necessary to amend the Constitution, is it possible that the Thirteenth, Fourteenth, and Fifteenth Amendments could themselves be repealed someday in a return to slavery and discrimination. Who would be the slaves in such a society? Blacks? Jews? Homosexuals? Christians? Atheists? What man has decreed is effective only as long as the decree has the support of the majority, the law, or the powerful—that is, unless the decree has come from outside the world. History reveals that the only truly effective, unalterable law is the transcendent higher law of God.

The higher law decrees that all races of people are of the human kind, descended from the first human, Adam (Acts 17:26). Furthermore, the scriptural higher law says, "There is neither Jew nor Greek, there is neither slave nor free man, there is neither male nor female, for you are all one in Christ Jesus" (Galatians 3:28). Racial equality is established by the very Creator of the races and is not subject to amendment, dissent, or negotiation. From God's absolute standard of justice, the laws and deeds of men can be truly judged.

2. Higher law presents the divinely ordained means of guiding individuals and society through the chaos into stability and fulfillment.

Without an established destination, a journey is little more than aimless wandering. When people fail to realize their purpose in life, confusion and chaos are inescapable. Without an established direction, the odds against reaching a meaningful goal are astronomical. God's higher law provides both direction and destination for the sojourners of this world. Scripture provides His way out of the miry clay and onto the solid Rock (Psalm 40:2).

Biblically based higher law contains all the help and insight necessary to follow the divinely appointed path. The way for individuals and society to escape the moral chaos of this age is simple: "All Scripture is inspired by God and profitable for teaching, for reproof, for correction, for training in righteousness" (2 Timothy 3:16).

Teaching is the means to instruct people and society concerning God's pathway through the chaos. *Reproof* is the use of God's higher law to show individuals and society when they've fallen off the righteous pathway. *Correction* is the use of higher law to get individuals and the culture back onto the divinely ordained pathway. *Training in righteousness* is the way in which higher law can keep individuals and society on the righteous pathway and out of the chaos.

3. Higher law provides perfect standards of judgment, as well as grace, mercy, and forgiveness for those who fall short of God's standards.

The Scripture makes it clear that there are no human beings who are perfectly righteous (Psalm 14:1, Romans 3:10). Everyone falls short of the glory of God (Romans 3:23). There are those who, by their own efforts, hope to achieve perfect righteousness. Isaiah the prophet said, "All of us have become like one who is unclean, and all our righteous deeds are like a filthy garment" (Isaiah 64:6).

Those who insist on attempting a self-accomplished, works righteousness are generally unaware of God's standard of judgment. God's higher law says that "whoever keeps the whole law and yet stumbles in one point, he has become guilty of all" (James 2:10). Furthermore, the higher law's perfect standard of judgment is reflected in the Person of Jesus Christ (Romans 2:16). In order to satisfy God's requirements of good works, all one has to do is live a life as perfect as Jesus Christ—no sin, with everything done properly and for the right reason.

The futility of trying to comply with God's standard of perfection is obvious. If there only existed this one approach to pleasing God, then everyone would be hopelessly doomed. But the same higher law which indicts and condemns us for our shortfalls also leads us to the One who is able to forgive our failures. The apostle Paul wrote to the Galatians, "The Law has become our tutor to lead us to Christ, that we may be justified by faith" (Galatians 3:24). Both individuals and society as a whole can be delivered through the redeeming power of Christ, which is shown by the higher law to be the only means of salvation.

The Results of a Higher Law Practice

If our chaotic world would take the time to consider God's higher law, then the confusion which results from moral relativity would begin to vanish. Those who formerly had no standard other than personal preference to judge actions of themselves and others would be given the means to make accurate and meaningful evaluations of the deeds of men. The consequences of perpetuating a moral relativity would be similar to what would happen if our standards of weights and measures suddenly vanished. The heavy-thumbed butcher would no longer have to cheat his customers. He would merely have to arbitrarily say, "This is three pounds." Without a fixed standard by which to judge weight, who could argue? Everything related to weight and measurement would be a matter of opinion. The effect of this upon doing business would be catastrophic. Why, though, do we accept the argument in the ethical and moral arenas that nothing is fixed, everything is a matter of opinion, and there are no absolutes?

God's higher law, then, is able to regulate both the sinner and the sinful culture. Not only are perfect standards presented so that there can be accurate evaluations of how well we are doing, but there are also the means to be forgiven for failures. But the beginning point must be our willingness, individually and collectively, to see ourselves as God sees us and then allow God to correct our deficiencies. If we stop short of the corrective power of the law and grace, we are mere "hearers of the word":

> For if anyone is a hearer of the word and not a doer, he is like a man who looks at his natural face in a mirror; for once he has looked at himself and gone away, he has immediately forgotten what kind of person he was (James 1:23,24).

Once we have recognized through gazing intently at God's perfect law that we need to make changes in our lives, then our task is to allow the Word of God to direct us in doing what God requires:

> But one who looks intently at the perfect law,
> the law of liberty, and abides by it, not having
> become a forgetful hearer but an effectual doer,
> this man shall be blessed in what he does (James
> 1:25).

In his book *Saints Alive*, James Adair relays the story of
Ernest Gaither, a young man facing death in the electric
chair.

> I'm ... just 23 years of age, but I'm ready to
> go, you see. Why if my number were up this very
> minute, I'd be ready to meet God. Just this week I
> had a dream that I'll carry with me to the chair. I
> was on my way to heaven. Jesus was with me. He
> asked me why I was going so fast. I told him I was
> eager to get there. Some folks might think that's
> strange talk from a man who came to jail an
> atheist. But that's the way I feel.
>
> Not long after I was placed behind bars ... a
> woman ... invited me to attend a prisoners'
> gospel service. I ... laughed at her. Why, I don't
> even believe there's a God. Actually I felt so
> sinful that I didn't want to know about God,
> even if He existed.
>
> The woman said, "If you don't believe in
> God ... before you go to sleep tonight ask Him
> to awaken you at any time; then ask Him to
> forgive you."[1]

Gaither didn't go to the service, but asked God to
wake him at 2:45 A.M. "if you're real." After sleeping
soundly, Gaither awoke and asked a prison guard the
time. "Fifteen to three." Gaither climbed down from his
cot and asked God to be merciful to him, "an evil murderer and sinner." Gaither said, "He saved me that night I
know. I've believed on His son Jesus ever since. . . . God
had saved me from my sins."

Peter Tanis, a prison missionary, tells the rest of the story which occurred some months after Ernest Gaither's conversion.

> I was admitted to Ernest's cell about an hour before midnight. . . . as I entered, Ernest smiled and greeted me. . . . Ernest leaned forward as I read: "For me to live is Christ, and to die is gain. . . . For I am in a straight betwixt two, having a desire to depart and to be with Christ, which is far better." A moment later a black hood was slipped over his head and he began the last mile. At each side were guards, both noticeably nervous. Ernest sensed it. "What are you fellows shaking for? I'm not afraid." [2]

At 12:03 A.M. the first of three powerful electrical shocks flashed through Ernest Gaither's body. By 12:15 five doctors had confirmed him dead.

Tanis concludes, "But I knew the real Ernest Gaither still lived—only his body was dead. As I left the prison, I thought of the verse he liked so well: 'For me to live is Christ, but to die is gain.' "[3]

The higher law, as a mirror of God's perfection, reveals to us how unclean we have become and exactly where it is that we need to be cleansed. But mirrors don't clean. Instead, they make us aware of our condition so that we might pursue the means by which we can be cleansed. The law shows us that our souls need to be washed through and through. By doing so, it guides us to the One God has appointed to deal with personal and society's sin and failure. It is Jesus Christ who died for the sins of the world so that the sting of the law could be overcome by the forgiveness He offers to all who believe. If we allow the perfect law of God to set the course for our life and permit the grace of God to restore us when we fall off the righteous path, then the chaos of a confused age will not affect our attaining the abundant life Christ offers. Who can withstand the crashing waves in the sea of uncertainty but those who have an anchor for their souls?

> O death, where is your victory? O death, where is your sting? The sting of death is sin, and the power of sin is the law; but thanks be to God who gives us the victory through our Lord Jesus Christ (1 Corinthians 15:55-57).

5

The Decline of Education

The United States Department of Education estimates that there are 24 million functionally illiterate people in America who have been through the educational system. These are not people who have never attended school. Instead, these are individuals who for the most part have spent eight to twelve years in public schools. Is there a connection between the miserable failure of American public education and the secularization of America? The evidence seems to make a strong argument for such a conclusion.

Ronald Nash tells the story of a fifth-grade teacher in Mobile, Alabama, who held a Master of Education degree from an American teachers' college. The teacher sent a note home to one of her students' parents, which read exactly as follows:

> Scott is dropping in his studies he acts as if he
> dont care. Scott want pass in his assignment at
> all, he a had a poem to learn and he fell to do it.

No wonder Scott acts as if he "dont care" (sic) and "fell" (sic) to do his assignment. And no wonder students are functionally illiterate when teachers, even with master's degrees, are functionally illiterate!

Teaching the Morality of Secularism

How does a secular society which embraces moral relativity and nihilism ("belief in nothing") teach values? Although there are numerous ideas which have been put forth in attempts to fill the moral vacuum created by secularism, the only matter upon which there is universal agreement is that "traditional values" have got to go.

The dean of the Harvard School of Education, Theodore Sizer, and his wife, Nancy, coedited a 1970 book entitled *Moral Education*. In it they condemn what they call the morality of "the Christian gentleman," "the American prairie," and the McGuffy *Reader*. Teachers who still use a grading system are accused of being hypocrites. The editors claim that every author in their anthology agreed there was no place left in America's new schools for "the old morality."

Can secular education actually believe that "the old morality" is the problem and that moral relativity is the solution? Kenneth Gangel in the book *Schooling Choices*, edited by H. Wayne House, quotes an extreme statement made by a Harvard University professor of educational psychiatry at a 1973 teachers' seminar to indicate how far some will go:

> Every child in America entering school at the age of five is mentally ill, because he comes to school with certain allegiances toward our founding fathers, toward our elected officials, toward his parents, toward a belief in a supernatural entity. It's up to you teachers to make all of these sick children well by creating the international children of the future.[1]

There is indeed a battle for the mind taking place today. Unfortunately, secularism has been winning battle after battle while the church continues to raise the walls which isolate her from her culture. The battle in education, as stated by professor of psychology Paul Vitz from New York University, is "between those who are religious and support traditional values and those who are secular and advocate antitraditional or modernistic values." Could the battle lines be drawn any clearer? To the victor go the hearts and minds of tomorrow's leaders.

The legacy of Christianity's retreat from education includes the creation of a public school monopoly controlled by secularists, a resultant moral chaos, and a functionally illiterate generation. Graduates of the present system are steeped in nihilistic thinking but aren't too sure they've had their non-values "clarified." The "values clarification" movement has been stripping away vestiges of moral absolutes which undergirded the tremendous prosperity of early America. This popular movement, according to philosopher Christina Sommers, is controlled by people whose approach to morality is without content:

> They are convinced that traditional middle-class morality is at best useless and at worst pernicious, and they have confidence in the new morality that is to replace the old and in the novel techniques to be applied to this end.[2]

Without moral absolutes, secular education encourages children to make moral choices among many options without regard to absolutes. What have we come to? As Gangel says:

> Is lying acceptable? Is stealing permissible? Should premarital sex be approved? Well, it depends. Situations differ. If young people have clarified their own value systems and have chosen to do or not to do these things, education has been achieved.[3]

In his book *The Closing of the American Heart,* Ronald Nash, professor of philosophy and religion at Western Kentucky University, says regarding parental apathy toward "values-clarification" programs:

> It is time to question the common sense of families who turn the education of their children over to people who might have felt right at home teaching values-clarification to the guards in the Nazi death camps.[4]

The Fountainhead of Secularism

How has twentieth-century public education been influenced to become the leading promoter of moral relativity and secularism? Our current public education system is the legacy of John Dewey (1859-1952). Dewey's system combined relativism, secularism, and humanism into a position called "instrumentalism." For Dewey, thinking was merely an *instrument* used to solve problems. "Truth" to Dewey was an idea that worked. Hence, Dewey's system is sometimes called "pragmatism."

What were the values of this man who has shaped the present public education system? According to Dewey:

> Faith in the prayer-hearing God is an unproved and outmoded faith. There is no God and there is no soul. Hence, there are no needs for the props of traditional religion. With dogma and creed excluded, then immutable truth is dead and buried. There is no room for fixed, natural law or moral absolutes.[5]

It is difficult to find a clearer expression of "moral relativity" than Dewey's statement. Dewey's ideas became the prevailing educational philosophy, and public education adopted his system. What has the effect been? Richard

M. Weaver in his book *Visions of Order* presents the assumptions which dominate public education today:

> There is no such thing as a body of knowledge which reflects the structure of reality and which everyone therefore needs to learn. Knowledge is viewed as an instrumentality which is true or false according to the way ... it serves the need of the individual. ... There is no final knowledge about anything. The truths of yesterday are the falsehoods of today and the truths of today will be the falsehoods of tomorrow.[6]

Is it no wonder that parents who provide godly instruction at home for their children find that public schools undermine their efforts? How can biblical absolutes compete with moral relativity when public schools present parents as black-hatted authority figures, purveyors of the "falsehoods of today"?

Teaching Teachers Secular Dogma

The secularizing of our age has been greatly accelerated through the public education system. It is in the classroom where the effects of secularism are the greatest. Teachers are the ones ultimately responsible for inculcating youth with ideas, values, and principles which will shape students into tomorrow's adults. And who are these teachers, the equippers of our children, who occupy the most prominent role in the secular sanctuary of learning known as the classroom? For the most part these are decent people who have themselves been educated by a system rife with secular, antitraditional values. To insure against holdouts from the traditional morality of the past, today's teacher is further "prepared" for teaching through teachers' college. These colleges have institutionalized socialism, secularism, and moral relativity. As Samuel Blumenfeld says:

A network of teachers' colleges—like a system of religious seminaries—has been built to train all of those who would become professionals in the educational establishment. In these colleges future teachers and administrators are indoctrinated in the dogma of the public religion.[7]

Reginald Damerell sums up the problem in the title of his book *Education's Smoking Gun: How Teachers' Colleges Have Destroyed Education in America.* Damerell says, "Empty credentials are all that any school or department of education in any university in the United States gives to its graduates. The education field is devoid on intellectual content, has no body of knowledge of its own and acts as if bodies of knowledge do not exist in other university departments."[8]

What has the Dewey system produced, with its brave new secular approach to education? As to teachers themselves, the data are disconcerting at best and shocking at worst. In 1983, teachers in Houston, Texas, were required to take a competency test. The results of the test which included standard reading skills, mathematics, and writing—were abysmal. Sixty-two percent of the teachers failed the reading portion of the test, 46 percent flunked the math section, while 26 percent failed the writing exam. Added to this is the alarming fact that 763 of the 3200 teachers who took the tests cheated![9]

The condition of public education today must be, at least in part, viewed as the legacy of non-involvement in education by Christians. The horror of secularist-bred illiteracy is tempered by the church's sin of omission in abandoning education to the social engineers. There must be an understanding of both the problems of public education and the solutions.

Educational Activism on the Part of Christians

Solutions to the crisis in public education include: first, *active participation by believers in the educational process.* An essential starting point for parents of children in public school (and recommended for those without children in public school) is knowing firsthand the teachers of their children and the principals of their schools. Parent/teacher meetings are designed for interaction and can properly be used not only to determine *what* is being taught but *why* (i.e., what are the goals and *purposes* of the curriculum). Parents and nonparents alike can get the best feel for the strengths and weaknesses of a school through such first-hand contact.

Another important area of participation is the parent/teacher association (PTA) or parent/teacher organization (PTO). Your ideas and concerns can be shared both publicly and privately with fellow parents and concerned citizens. These contacts can become the seed of change through informing others of the perceived needs in the educational system and recruiting like-minded people in the battle for necessary change.

There are tremendous opportunities to support helpful programs and oppose harmful ones through participating in school-board meetings. How can a school board properly gauge the success of its programs without feedback from the public? It is both a privilege and responsibility for parents to voice their feelings and concerns. Some people will even feel called to a long-term commitment in solving the public education crisis. If you are such a person, why not run for the school board?

Active participation at some level of the public education process is a key to regaining control of the moral compass of our culture. The fields are ready to harvest, but unfortunately the laborers are few. What can you offer?

Second, *support efforts to break the public school monopoly*. In an age where "choice" has become a god, choice has been dethroned in the area of public education. The public school monopoly has carefully prevented competition from forcing it to become efficient. For those who opt out and send their children to private schools (or home school), there is a double economic burden: First, taxes are extracted which pay for unused public education, and second, the additional costs of private education, which are not tax-deductible, are personally borne.

One positive solution is tuition tax credits for those who send their children to private schools or who home school. Under this plan the additional costs of pursuing parental choice in education are, at least in part, offset by providing either a tax credit or an income tax deduction for private or home school expenses. There should be some relief from the extra economic burden of parents who choose nonpublic education for their children.

Another means of breaking the public school monopoly is providing choice *within* public education. This means giving parents the choice to send their children to whichever public school they choose, irrespective of district boundaries. If parents had such a choice, then public schools, just like private ones, would be forced to either be competitive or fold up. The incentive for efficiency is lacking under the present system. If a public school's survival depended on its achievement of results, the quality of public education could change overnight. A by-product of this proposal is that educators could get back to educating instead of spending so much time working on political agendas designed to further protect their monopoly.

Tuition tax credits, competition among public schools, and other means of providing meaningful "choice" to parents will only occur if parents speak up. Our state and federal representatives are the ones who ultimately can deliver the means to break the public school monopoly. Only through concerted efforts by outspoken parents will the legislature ever be willing to resist the pressure of the well-organized, well-financed, and powerful public education lobby.

Third, *support the Christian school movement.* Christian schools, even for those parents who can afford them, are not the panacea of education. However, Christian schools provide a necessary and helpful alternative to the public school monopoly. The teaching of a positive, biblically based morality is a cornerstone of Christian schools. Public schools, however, are philosophically bound to a pragmatic, utilitarian ethic which presents a morality based on expedience (e.g., "Don't have premarital sex because it might result in pregnancy or disease. If you do have sex, use a condom to avoid the consequences."). Under such an ethical system of moral relativity, if one can avoid the consequences of illicit sex, illegal drugs, or even criminal conduct, no significant reason remains for refraining from these activities. Any appeal to what is "right" is a mere subjective, traditional assertion, without a solid basis.

Christian schools, on the other hand, can present biblical absolutes which form the basis for a Christian ethic. Instead of appealing to human opinion as to what is right, the revealed Word of God provides a prescriptive foundation for conduct: God has spoken about what constitutes right and wrong.

Beyond the spiritual advantage of teaching biblical absolutes, Christian schools consistently maintain an academic advantage over their public school counterparts. This may help explain why public school teachers tend to send their own children to private schools in a percentage much higher than the general population. Would most people eat in a restaurant whose chefs choose to eat elsewhere? When public school teachers send their own children to private schools, it is clear testimony to the relative inferiority of the public school system. Although not all public schools are inferior, nor are all Christian schools superior, on the average Christian schools consistently outperform public schools on standardized achievement tests. Given the fact that per-pupil spending is approximately three times more for public schools than for Christian schools, it is crucial for those who are concerned about the crisis in public education to philosophically and, when possible, materially support the Christian school option.

Finally, *support the home school advantage.* Despite the historical pattern of parents teaching their children at home, some states continue with attempts to criminalize home schooling. Compulsory attendance laws which help enforce the public school monopoly are used to deny parents the legitimate choice of educating their own children as they see fit. As with Christian schools, the rapidly growing home schooling movement typically has produced academic results superior to public schools. While home schooling may never be the practice of the majority, it has proven its place in education through the positive results it has achieved. Thus, the home school option should be understood and supported by anyone who is concerned about the crisis in our public schools.

Christian involvement in education is a necessity if Christianity is to reemerge as a dominant force in society. For education to be rebuilt, individuals must be willing to pay the price. Jesus said, "For which one of you, when he wants to build a tower, does not first sit down and calculate the cost, to see if he has enough to complete it?" (Luke 14:28). It's time to count the cost, find the means, and pay the price.

6

The Secularization of Law

The importance of law as a means of protecting the moral values of society has been discovered the hard way by millions of God-fearing people. Disinterest and unfamiliarity with the legal system during the early and mid-twentieth century has resulted in churches reeling from the societal and personal effects of changes in the law. While the attitude prevailed that "ministry" was something done behind a pulpit or on a mission field, law was seen as a hairsplitting profession suited for the carnal and greedy ("Woe to you lawyers as well!"—Luke 11:46).

Law in the United States and British Commonwealth countries is derived from English "common law." This refers to the decisions of judges for countless generations when considering cases of civil and criminal law. English common law is rooted in the notion of moral absolutes, which it obtained from the Bible. Every law student has noticed the assumptions of biblical morality and Judeo-Christian values which pervade case law. From before the time of Sir William Blackstone (eighteenth-century England) up to and beyond the time of Benjamin Cardozo (early twentieth-century America), the Scriptures are liberally quoted in support of judicial decisions. But despite the obvious Christian influence in the lives and judicial opinions of leading scholars such as Blackstone in the seventeenth century and Harvard's Simon Greenleaf in the nineteenth century, the twentieth century shows a departure from the Bible-based moral absolutes as the cornerstone of legal decisions.

How did it happen that a country founded on Judeo-Christian principles developed laws hostile toward God and the Bible? While Christians were busy elsewhere, the religious heritage of our country was gradually replaced with a judicially imposed secularism. For the church to understand the effect of her isolation from social involvement, it is necessary to recall what the United States used to stand for and how secularism crept in through the Supreme Court. The legacy of noninvolvement by Christians is graphically illustrated by the history of the secularization of American law.

The United States of America was established as a country on July 4, 1776. The first step in the birth of this new nation was to assert its sovereignty. This was done through a founding document called the "Declaration of Independence." What assumptions and values underlie this "birth certificate" of the United States? The declaration justifies dissolving America's political dependence upon the British by asserting that "the laws of nature and of nature's God" compel such a separation. In further elaborating upon the grounds for establishing independence, the declaration refers to "self-evident truths." These "truths" were as axiomatic to the Founding Fathers of America as the understanding that fire is hot and water is wet. What were the irrefutable assumptions of these men as codified in the declaration?

- all men are created equal.
- they are endowed by their Creator with certain unalienable rights.

- among these Creator–endowed rights are
  life, liberty, and the pursuit of happiness.

The declaration further makes reference to the signatories' reliance on "Divine Providence." The "self-evident" truths spelled out in the declaration are indicative of the biblically based, Judeo-Christian assumptions of the eighteenth century. Just as the declaration speaks of the self-evident truth that "all men are created equal" by a Creator God, so the Bible says that the knowledge of the Creator is evident within man "because that which is known about God is evident within them; for God made it evident to them" (Romans 1:19).

The declaration makes clear that it is the Creator who has endowed human beings with "unalienable rights." These "moral absolutes" include the right to "life, liberty and the pursuit of happiness." In the more than two centuries since the Declaration of Independence, the departure from biblical assumptions has altered the notion of moral absolutes. Instead of a Bible-based, Creator-based set of values, a creeping secularism has invaded legal, political, and moral thinking. The result has been a moral relativity which relies upon consensus of human opinion, expediency, and utilitarian ethics rather than the moral absolutes derived from a transcendent God. In terms of the effect of this departure upon law, recent United States Supreme Court decisions indicate how far the judicial mainstream in America has strayed from its roots. Many of the self-evident truths declared by the Founding Fathers are not only called into question, they are flat out rejected. Along came *Roe v. Wade* in 1973, and all of a sudden the church rediscovered the effect of law on Christianity and its practices.

The Legacy of Secularization of the Law

Roe v. Wade opened the eyes of millions of people to the need of having a judiciary that upholds the sanctity of human life, including the life of the unborn. Since the 1973 decision, tremendous efforts have been spent chipping away at *Roe*, with hopes of eventually seeing the case overturned. Had Christians "occupied" the legal profession in the early and mid-twentieth century, the complexion of the Supreme Court in 1973 might have been different. Had more people with biblical perspectives been on the Court, it's likely that *Roe* would have been decided differently. The time spent trying to overturn *Roe* could have been used to reach society for Christ. Instead it's been years of "catch-up." As the saying goes, "An ounce of prevention is worth a pound of cure." The time has arrived for preventive action so that law is not permitted to restrict or undermine the mission of the church.

School Prayer Struck Down

The New York board of regents had prepared a "non-denominational" prayer for use in state public schools. The prayer read: "Almighty God, we acknowledge our dependence upon Thee, and we beg Thy blessings upon us, our parents, our teachers and our country." A local school board directed that the prayer be recited daily by each class. Parents of a number of children challenged the practice, claiming it was "contrary to the beliefs, religions, or religious practices of both themselves and their children." New York's highest court upheld the practice, so long as the schools did not compel any student to join in the prayer over a parent's objection.

Despite the fact that the prayer was denominationally neutral and that its observation on the part of the student was voluntary, the United States Supreme Court, in *Engel v. Vitale* (1962), held the practice to be unconstitutional. Justice Hugo Black's majority opinion stated that the First Amendment's establishment clause ("Congress shall make no law respecting an establishment of religion. . . .") "must at least mean that [it] is no part of the business of government to compose a part of a religious program carried on by government."

One irony of the *Engel* decision is that each session of the United States Supreme Court is opened with the clerk reciting the prayer: "God save the United States of America and this honorable Court." Furthermore, despite the fact, as Justice Potter Stewart said in his dissent in *Engel*, "We are a religious people whose institutions presuppose a Supreme Being," it became illegal to permit class prayers to the Creator mentioned in the Declaration of Independence.

School-Sponsored Bible Reading Struck Down

The state of Pennsylvania had a law prescribing that "at least 10 verses from the Holy Bible shall be read, without comment, at the opening of each school day." The law provided that "any child shall be excused from such Bible reading or attending such Bible reading, upon written request of parent or guardian."

By the year 1963 the statute had been on the books for 50 years. Despite this, the Unitarian parents of two students at Abington High School sued the school district, claiming the practice violated the "establishment clause" of the First Amendment to the U.S. Constitution, which provides that "Congress shall make no law respecting the establishment of religion."

The U.S. Supreme Court in an 8-1 decision agreed that the Pennsylvania law and a similar Maryland law were unconstitutional. The reasoning of the Court is most enlightening. Writing the majority opinion, Justice Tom Clark asked what was the "purpose and primary effect" of the laws in question. If it was to advance or inhibit religion, the laws are barred by the Constitution. Justice Clark wrote that there must be a "secular purpose" for the laws. The promotion of moral values didn't qualify! Furthermore, excusing students opposed to such practices was not seen as a defense to the Constitutional problems raised by the Court majority. For them, the laws mandating Bible reading breached the neutrality of the state. The Court spoke of the threat that "today's trickling stream may become tomorrow's raging torrent unless it is stopped." How sadly ironic that the Court's decision contributed to the raging torrent of humanism. Justice Clark considered such a possibility. However, he rejected the argument that, unless religious exercises are permitted, a "religion of secularism" is established in schools. History has unfortunately proven Justice Clark to be dead wrong.

Is It Reasonable to Counsel from the Bible?

The *Nalley v. Grace Community Church of the Valley* case involved the question of whether pastors and churches have judicially created duties imposed upon them when it comes to counseling parishioners. The plaintiffs in this California case alleged that there is a professional counseling standard by which clergy must abide. The standard was alleged to include a duty to act reasonably under the circumstances and a duty to require the proper level of psychological training on the part of lay church counselors.

Someone may ask, What's wrong with a duty to act "reasonably"? One should hope that all people, both within and without the church, would act "reasonably." But the important issue is, "Reasonable by whose definition?" If a pastor or church counselor must employ principles of secular, Freudian counseling to be considered "reasonable," then the state has determined how the church must practice her calling. If the Bible cannot be used as the sole rule of faith and practice by pastors, then the state has breached the First Amendment of the United States Constitution, which forbids state action from prohibiting the free exercise of religion.

The plaintiff in the *Nalley* case essentially wanted to replace the church's practice of good faith reliance on the Bible for solutions to personal problems with reliance on secular psychology standards. Anything less was alleged to be below the standard of care a pastor was required to exercise. Briefly stated, the plaintiffs claimed that failing to exercise this "standard of care" constituted "clergy malpractice."

Again, who is to determine the "standard of care" a pastor must exercise? And should the pastor and church be liable for monetary damages if a pastor's care falls below this "standard"? Whether it is "reasonable" for pastors and churches to rely solely on the Bible for counseling is not a question the state nor the courts are permitted to ask. If it were otherwise, the state, a judge, or a jury could stand in *judgment* of the reasonableness and validity of religion. Fortunately, in the *Nalley* case the court held, "It is not for this court, or any court in the United States, to pass judgment on the beliefs of . . . any church."

The Ten Commandments Outlawed

In 1978 the state of Kentucky wished to present to schoolchildren the heritage of the American legal system. A law was passed which required the Ten Commandments to be posted in public school classrooms. The law also required the following statement on the posters:

> The secular application of the Ten Commandments is clearly seen in its adoption as the fundamental legal code of Western civilization and the Common Law of the United States.

In 1980 the U.S. Supreme Court struck down the Kentucky law, again agreeing that it violated the First Amendment's prohibition of the establishment of religion. The Court said that the Ten Commandments were "plainly religious" and may induce the schoolchildren to read, meditate upon, perhaps to venerate and obey the commandments. Apparently the Code of Hammurabi, the Napoleonic Code, and other significant examples of legal tradition could be posted legally. But the line was drawn at the display of the legal and moral principles codified in Exodus 20:1-17 because they might be taken seriously.

Reversing the Trend

Why has there been a systematic removal of religious expression from public life? Why has religion in general, and Christianity in particular, been assailed through the courts? Why has there been a tremendous rise in litigation affecting organizations such as churches which were traditionally exempt from secular law? These questions are inseparably united, and at least three possible answers exist.

First, the rise of secularism has brought about an increase in hostility toward things religious. Second, the courts have become a place for those intolerant of religion (if not hateful toward God) to attempt indirectly what they can't do directly: attack the belief in a Creator to whom we are all accountable. Third, the increasingly litigious nature of our society has prompted people to file lawsuits against anyone on even the most trivial of matters. The perception is that churches are "deep pockets" who have become rich through oppression, exploitation, and abuse of tax-exempt status. This notion has made churches an increasingly popular target for lawsuits. With a misguided zeal, antichurch litigants often see themselves as modern-day Robin Hoods, who file lawsuits instead of fire arrows, in order to take from the "rich" churches and give to the poor.

Even though the law unwittingly endorses an antireligious, intolerant secularism, all is not lost. The same insidious secularism which inspired the changes in the way the law views religion can be replaced with what used to dominate our society: Judeo-Christian values. When committed, knowledgeable Christians actively challenge the assumptions of our secular age and begin winning the battle for the hearts and minds of our civilization, the effects will be felt across all facets of society, including the law. We should begin with efforts to bring the law back to its stated position of "benevolent neutrality" toward religion—a vast improvement over today's pervasive antireligious hostility. This and more can be accomplished if people of faith understand the problems with the law and pursue the solutions. The law should not be an obstacle to changing our culture, but a vehicle: "But we know that the Law is good, if one uses it lawfully" (1 Timothy 1:8).

7

A Brave New Secular Future

What happens to a secular society left unchecked by the restraints of moral absolutes? Whenever fallen human beings are given unfettered discretion to guide culture, the result is inevitable disaster. History is replete with examples of tyrants, oppressors, and terrorists who epitomize the notion of "man's inhumanity toward fellow-man." These serve as reminders of the consequences of lawlessness and godlessness. In our present secular age, the prospects for anything other than societal chaos are grim.

The specter of a brave new secular age includes the horror of what might happen in an era marked by shifting, uncertain standards. Reliance upon the capacity for good within the human heart—a solution proposed by only the extremely optimistic—is the equivalent of playing societal Russian roulette. Jeremiah the prophet said, "The heart is more deceitful than all else and is desperately sick; who can understand it?" (Jeremiah 17:9). Albert Einstein, commenting on the threat of atomic warfare, asked, "What are we afraid of? The power of the atom bomb, or the force of evil

77

within the human heart?" The more things change, the more they stay the same.

Evil: An Alternative Life-style

It has been said, "All that is necessary for evil to triumph is for good people to do nothing." Another way, however, for evil to triumph is to excuse, justify, or deny the existence of evil. Those who champion a cultural agnosticism, denying that there are absolute answers, are adept at explaining away evil. Whether due to environmental determinism, genetics, or too many Twinkies, personal responsibility and accountability are explained away. To quote the pseudophilosopher and mass murderer Charles Manson, "If God is one, what is evil?" Indeed, what is evil?

In a morally relative universe, as one poet said, "Sin we have explained away. None the less, the sinners stay." With all the prattle about values being in the eye of the beholder, one would think that such insight into the question of evil would free people to do "good." Unfortunately, if "evil" is a fabrication of religion and culture, a mere label for behavior caused by a number of complex factors, then "good" must also be explained away. Yet virtually no one is willing to do away with good. Strange inconsistencies, indeed!

With the dubious acceptance of cultural agnosticism and moral relativity, society has begun its headlong plunge into the abyss of cultural chaos. What direction are we headed, and what frightening scenarios can we anticipate, given the current trends? Although no human can say with certainty what ominous developments loom ahead for humanity, drastic changes in human behavior are either being discussed or have actually begun. It is from these that we can project what the future will be like. The primary obstacle to these changes taking place is the success of Christians holding back the forces producing the change. Without an effective, relevant church influencing society, the following predictions are virtually certain to become commonplace in the world.

Defining and Qualifying the Term "Life"

In an age where there exists a clear consensus on the definition of "death" (when at least two of three of the vital signs of heartbeat, respiration, or brain waves are missing), it is remarkable that a debate continues on the definition of "life." Adding to the confusion are those who qualify the term "life" with words describing its perceived use to society or its capacity to enjoy existence. The classic example is the expression "quality of life." Quality by whose definition? And what if a person doesn't measure up to some arbitrary standard of "quality"?

Adding confusion to the debate over "life" is the denial of any special significance to human life other than its intelligence and capacity to plunder the earth. Environmentalists and others have adopted "Star Trek" terminology, referring to human beings as merely one of many "life-forms." This evolutionary view of man, which rejects the idea of humans having been uniquely created in the image of God, raises some interesting questions.

For example, what if some higher intelligence came to earth and decided that humans constituted tasty morsels for the aliens' palates? What would morally prevent these superintelligent extraterrestrials from munching on Homo sapiens as we munch on cows, chickens, and fish? The answer is "Nothing," since in such relativistic, evolutionary thinking, cows, chickens, and fish are to human beings what we are to aliens: less intelligent "life-forms."

Could the recent increase in vegetarian philosophy be explained at least in part by the guilt of eating biological relatives and by the fear of similarly being eaten by something higher up the evolutionary ladder? Fortunately, for those who believe that man was specially created in the moral and spiritual image of God and was given dominion over creation, such questions of alien appetites are absurd. Such fanciful and speculative discussions are better left to the "Twilight Zone" or to Hindu philosophers who believe (at least they did before the invention of the microscope) that it's wrong to kill any living thing, including bugs.

With evolutionary assumptions replacing the biblical concept of mankind's uniqueness in God's program, human life has become the cause of global problems, rather than possessing the solution. The very survival of planet Earth is said to be in jeopardy due to factors such as overpopulation, pollution, and the threat of nuclear holocaust. Since man is the problem, how do we eliminate the problem?

Solutions to the Problem of Man

Eighteenth-century British economist Thomas Malthus was especially concerned with overpopulation. He concluded that populations will always increase faster than food supplies and that, therefore, hunger will always exist among the poorest populations. Malthus did, however, think that natural factors such as disease, famine, and wars kept the population restricted. Although Malthusian pessimism has largely been rejected, artificial means of limiting population are in the works.

The United States Supreme Court decision in *Roe v. Wade*, issued January 22, 1973, was a precursor to the rapid devaluation of life. The decision allowed abortions to legally take place up through the ninth month of pregnancy for any reason or for no reason. *Roe* effectively established a legal abortion industry in the United States, which has become nearly a billion-dollar-per-year enterprise, providing more than one and one-half million abortions annually. Presently, one out of three pregnancies ends in abortion, and abortion has become the most common surgical procedure performed today.

Abortion on demand, which ends the life of unborn human beings, is justified by asserting a woman's right to "choose." The convenience of the pregnant woman supersedes the right of the fetus to live, according to the Supreme Court. The *Roe* decision allowed the camel to get his nose inside the tent, and it is difficult to prevent him from progressing further.

Roe paved the way for the next step in the process of devaluing life through qualifications, redefinitions, and outright denial of the biological facts. The first salvo came in 1973, the same year as the *Roe* decision, when Nobel-prize-winner James Watson stated,

> If a child is not declared alive until three days after birth, then all parents could be allowed the choice only a few are given under the present system. The doctor could allow the child to die if the parents so choose and save a lot of misery and suffering. I believe this view is the only rational, compassionate attitude to have.[1]

Watson's view, a clear call for legal infanticide, permits parents a "choice." A living baby is treated worse than an undercooked steak at a restaurant. At least the steak can be sent back for more cooking to make it more acceptable. But a baby who fails to please the parents—perhaps due to being the wrong sex, too dark, too light, etc.—loses its one chance at life.

Another Nobel laureate, Francis Crick, said in 1978 that "no newborn infant should be declared human until it passes certain tests regarding its genetic endowment and that if it fails these tests it forfeits the right to live."[2] This idea of Crick, however, is not new. Those who lacked the required Aryan endowment in Nazi Germany forfeited their right to live. Adolph Hitler determined the criteria, and Jews automatically failed his test.

Fetal "Farming": The Profit/Loss of Conception

If one accepts the premise that unborn babies are not "persons," what prevents the harvesting of fetal tissue for research or transplantation? In an age where surrogacy has relegated motherhood to a contractual obligation, the specter looming on the horizon is "conceive for pay, abort for profit."

Research into the human immune system in the 1980s took a quantum leap when scientists found a way to transplant human immune cells into the bodies of mice. Through such transplants, diseases such as AIDS and leukemia can be observed and monitored throughout their course of infection. Experimental drugs are used to treat the diseases— a luxury unavailable if the host of the infection were a living human.

A moral dilemma arises, however. It was discovered that the best way to reproduce a human immune system in mice was through the use of human fetal tissue transplants. Fetal tissue has been determined to be superior for many reasons, including its adaptability to a new environment and rapid growth. The issue is whether it is ethical to use the tissue from aborted babies in these experiments. A National Institute of Health advisory committee determined in 1988 that it is "acceptable" for tissue from intentionally aborted fetuses to be used in medical research.

The committee, skirting the underlying issue of the morality of abortion, said:

> It is of moral relevance that human fetal tissue for research has been obtained from induced abortions. However, in light of the fact that abortion is legal and that the research in question is intended to achieve significant medical goals, the panel concludes that the use of such tissue is acceptable public policy.[3]

Since the legality of abortion is used to justify the use of the tissue from unborn humans in medical research, then if Nobel prizewinner Francis Crick has his way, we can substitute the word "infanticide" for "abortion." Arms, legs, brains, and internal organs of living, born human beings would merely be considered "spare parts" available for use in the pursuit of "significant medical goals." As in the case of aborted fetuses, consent of the victim is academic. Nonpersons have no capacity to consent.

In the evolutionary hierarchy of experimentation with human tissue, mature human beings become the aliens who feed on the "lower life-forms" of unborn and infant humanity. Without resorting to science fiction or New Age babble, there exists a perfectly good word which describes the essence of the practices: cannibalism. Is there any substantive difference between natives killing a person in the jungle versus researchers killing an unborn baby or infant in a laboratory in order to transplant the organs to another?

A convincing argument could be made even to those who hold to the biblical view of man that naturally miscarried or ectopic fetuses should be available for research and tissue transplantation. What began as a tragedy for grieving parents could become the comforting knowledge that their loss might be someone else's gain. One scientist, speaking to the National Institute of Health Committee, estimated the potential beneficiaries of transplanted fetal cells included 600,000 persons with diabetes; 500,000 with Parkinson's disease; 300,000 with spinal cord injuries; and at least 2 million with Alzheimer's disease. Would the use of naturally miscarried tissue to sustain life be worthy of moral absolution in the same way in which plane-crash survivors were absolved from their use of the flesh of deceased crash victims for lifesaving sustenance?

Whether one agrees with the brave new secular world's practice of using human tissue, there are ethical boundaries which have already been crossed. For example, there's the case of the Ohio woman, aged 49, whose 57-year-old husband was suffering from Parkinson's disease for nearly a decade. After hearing about the possibilities of using aborted fetus cells to assist Parkinson victims, the woman responded:

> I know it sounds terrible, but if I could become pregnant and have an abortion to help him, I would do it. It's not something I would want to do. But if he couldn't be helped any other way, I would do it. You've got to understand.

This is somebody you love so badly, I'd do anything to help him.

If it's morally right to use intentionally aborted fetuses (or murdered babies, a la Francis Crick) in experimentation and transplant, what's to keep "fetal farming" from becoming big business? According to a 1976 *Washington Post* story, between 1972 and 1974 D.C. General Hospital's obstetric and gynecology department sold the bodies and organs of unborn babies aborted by hysterotomy to Flow Labs of Rockville, Maryland. Flow, in turn, used tissue from the bodies to produce cell cultures which were sold to medical researchers. Seventy-five dollars was paid to D.C. General for each body supplied. The money received was spent on such items as a television set and soft drinks and cookies for visiting professors. The same hospital's pathology department had been involved in the sale of aborted babies' bodies for ten years, receiving $68,000 from commercial firms. With this type of precedent, what is next?[4]

New Concepts for Relationships

The term "marriage" is generally defined as "the state of, or relation between a man and woman who have become husband and wife." The elements of marriage, then, include a man, a woman, and a relationship which elevates them to the status of husband and wife. The relationship which constitutes "marriage" goes beyond the common practice of cohabitation.

For a true marriage to exist, a couple generally must comply with certain legal requirements, such as a marriage license. In order for a license to be issued, the man and woman must have the legal capacity to marry, which includes a legally unmarried status. They must also be consenting adults, or else minors with parental consent and/or court approval. Some jurisdictions recognize a "common law" marriage, in which the couple has cohabited for a certain period of time, such as seven years.

Perhaps one of the areas where the brave new secular future will undoubtedly see dramatic change is in definitions of words. Words which have remained the same since the beginning of civilization will take on meanings never before contemplated. The concept of marriage is a prime example.

The practice of heterosexual couples cohabiting without the benefit of marriage is on the increase. What used to be stigmatized as "living in sin" is now generally accepted. According to the Census Bureau, there are more than 2.5 million unmarried-couple households in the United States as of 1990—a 70 percent increase in ten years! Not only does this departure from belief in the wrongfulness of fornication demonstrate a morality by consensus, but it subtly denies the necessity of the institution of marriage. Beyond the street-level justification for abandoning the need for marriage ("Why buy a cow when milk is so cheap?") is the popular belief that "marriage is just a piece of paper."

When a divinely ordained institution (Genesis 2:24, Matthew 19:5) such as marriage is relegated to a mere document, far-reaching consequences result. Sexual relations are reduced to the fulfillment of biological urges, devoid of any spiritual significance. The biblical proscriptions against fornication are either explained away as archaic rules from bygone eras or else just plain ignored. The conception of children through cohabitation increasingly results in abortion. And the children that are born to unmarried couples are more apt to be confused, insecure, and unbonded to the natural parents. The brave new secular future is anticipated with glee by those who have willfully abandoned God's plan for the family. But people who opt for being the masters of their own fate will more than likely end up suffering from the hellish confusion that results from moral anarchy.

How ironic that millions of heterosexual couples have abandoned the need for legal marriage, while homosexual couples actively pursue legal recognition of their cohabitation! Various American cities have either proposed or already instituted "domestic partnership" laws which provide economic benefits for the cohabiting hetero and homosexual "partners" of city employees. In a society where biblical absolutes have been jettisoned with impunity, what is to prevent legal recognition of relationships formerly considered "immoral" or even "perverted"?

The brave new secular future will undoubtedly see the widespread, official recognition of homosexual relationships. Even now "marriages" are performed between couples of the same sex, with liberal clergy endorsing the "solemnizing" of such unions. In the name of progress and tolerance, the god of choice has prevailed. Now people are free to openly choose the poison of sexual practices which deviate from the monogamous, heterosexual model ordained in Scripture. Furthermore, official government sanction upon such practices is inevitably forthcoming.

If people ought to be free to choose their life-styles, then another dilemma arises: At what age should people be allowed to engage in consensual sexual activity? With common law, children under seven are conclusively presumed unable to form criminal intent. Children seven to fourteen are also presumed incapable of forming criminal intent, but the presumption is rebuttable by introducing sufficient evidence to establish that the youth knew what he was doing and that it was wrong. Children fourteen and older are treated as adults under common law.

Extrapolating from this, why can't children from seven to fourteen choose to participate in sexual conduct, and why aren't children fourteen and older absolutely able to engage in consensual sex? To the reasonable mind, sexuality is difficult enough for adults to deal with. Thus, immature children and adolescents have no business freely experimenting with sex. The potential for abuse of such children is staggering. Therefore, jurisdictions have enacted laws which make intercourse with women under an established "age of consent" a crime, without regard to whether the woman consented. Ironically, such "statutory rape" laws normally protect only females, although most jurisdictions now have strict laws preventing adults from sexual contact with children. Who could object to consent laws and statutory rape laws, since they offer such reasonable protection of children? NAMBLA, for one. Unlike the Boy Scouts, the North American Man-Boy Love Association (NAMBLA) is not a benevolent organization for the betterment of young boys. Instead, NAMBLA is an organization of pedophiles and dirty old men who want to eliminate consent laws. Why? Ostensibly to enable mature minors to legally decide for themselves whether they want to engage in sex, without regard to the age of the sexual partner. Could NAMBLA's goal have anything to do with the desire of pedophile homosexuals to prey on young boys without facing criminal prosecution? The fact that an organization such as NAMBLA is out in the open suggests how far a brave new secular society will go in tolerating "unconventional life-styles." With words expressing moral turpitude (such as "degenerate," "pervert," etc.) being dropped from common usage, and words such as "disgusting" expressing merely one's arbitrary personal opinion, the goals (both stated and hidden) of groups like NAMBLA are attainable within a few years.

Unconventional Parenthood

If society accepts the notion that homosexuality is merely an alternative life-style, then certain changes from existing social practices will occur. For example, why shouldn't practicing homosexuals be considered worthy candidates for adopting children? Also, what's wrong with homosexuals being awarded visitation rights or custody of children in divorce proceedings?

In 1988, a California appellate court overturned a judge's decision which restricted an eight-year-old boy from seeing his father, a practicing homosexual, whenever any other adult who was a "known homosexual" was present. The homosexual father, who was living with another man he described as his "life companion," challenged the restrictions. The appellate court said:

> The unconventional lifestyle of one parent or the opposing moral position of the parties ... do not provide an adequate basis for restricting visitation rights.[5]

California courts ruled in 1967 that a judge could not choose which parent would have physical custody of a child based solely on either parent's sexual preference. In 1988 the appellate court said that a parent's sexual conduct could be a factor in visitation only if there was "compelling evidence that such conduct has significant bearing upon the welfare of the child." If homosexuality is considered "acceptable," then how could homosexual practice *ever* have "significant bearing upon the welfare of the child"!

Without moral absolutes, secular courts call homosexuality merely an "unconventional life-style." What's to keep the practices of pedophilia, necrophilia, and bestiality from qualifying as "unconventional life-styles"? The slippery slope of moral relativity makes it extremely difficult, if not impossible, to maintain meaningful distinctions in aberrant sexual behavior. In fact, terms such as "aberrant," "deviant," and "perverted" are being supplanted by the word "unconventional"—an amoral word. The moral relativity of the present brave new secular world portends a future in which everyone does as they please. A parallel situation existed in Israel at the time of the Judges—a time when the nation was locked into a cycle of failure and corruption. The Scripture says, "In those days there was no king in Israel; everyone did what was right in his own eyes" (Judges 21:25). Today there is no God allowed within our culture; everyone does what seems right in his own eyes. Without God, there are no absolutes. And without absolutes, there is no right or wrong—only personal preferences.

In a culture which does away with biblical absolutes and traditional practices of morality, almost anything can happen. The practice of allowing homosexuals to adopt children—something that would have been unthinkable 20 years ago—is now being considered. Why not? It is logically consistent to extend the right to adopt children to homosexuals, since courts have granted custody of natural children to their homosexual parents in divorce proceedings. If homosexuals as a class are unfit as adoptive parents, they should be deemed unfit as custodial parents of their natural children. However, if they are not unfit per se to be custodial parents after a divorce (a view upheld by numerous courts), then homosexuals should not be unfit to be adoptive parents. Such a drift of social behavior and practices inevitably follows the abandoning of the anchor of moral absolutes. It's only a matter of time before the unthinkable becomes reality.

The Death of Judeo-Christian Assumptions

In the year 1878 the United States Supreme Court decided the case of *Reynolds v. United States*, in which the issue was whether or not a federal antipolygamy law was constitutional. The appellant, George Reynolds, was a Mormon. Reynolds had been indicted and convicted of bigamy, based upon a law which made bigamy a criminal offense in any federal territory under the jurisdiction of the federal government. Reynolds appealed his conviction, claiming that the right to practice polygamy was a tenet of the Mormon faith, thereby protected under the First Amendment's guarantee of freedom of religion. The Court said in response:

> Laws are made for the government of actions, and while they cannot interfere with mere religious belief and opinions, they may with practices. . . . So here, as a law . . . of the United States, it is provided that plural marriages shall not be

allowed. Can a man excuse his practices to the contrary because of his religious belief? To permit this would be to make the professed doctrines of religious belief superior to the law of the land, and in effect to permit every citizen to become a law unto himself.

The assumption of the Court in the *Reynolds* decision is that Congress can pass laws protecting the Judeo-Christian practice of heterosexual monogamy because the United States is built upon Judeo-Christian values. In the hundred-plus years since *Reynolds*, the United States has departed from its Judeo-Christian roots. In a world free from biblical absolutes, what state interest other than perpetuation of tradition is served by outlawing polygamy? Whether as a religious tenet or merely a chosen life-style, polygamy could easily become a lawful practice in a country which has abandoned its connection to biblical principles. The death of Judeo-Christian assumptions has set the stage for a brave new secular world.

In 1978 my wife and I were traveling in the Virgin Islands. After landing on the Island of St. Croix, we hailed a taxi to take us to our hotel. As we quickly noticed, the cars on St. Croix drove on the left-hand side of the road—the opposite of the United States. My wife asked the driver what it was like to drive "on the *wrong* side of the road." The driver slowly turned and exhorted: "It's not the *wrong* side of the road. It's the *left* side." As my wife slumped down in her seat, we learned a lesson in perspectives. From the perspective of those used to cars driving on the right, driving on the left was wrong. From the perspective of the taxi driver, driving on the left was merely different from what is practiced in the United States.

Since whether a country permits driving on the left side or the right side of the road is of no consequence (as long as everyone does it the same way!), there is no absolute right or wrong side for driving. Relative to the United States, islands like St. Croix and countries such as England and New Zealand have enacted driving habits which are different. As long as people in each island, country, or jurisdiction comply with the driving laws, traffic will flow smoothly. Otherwise, if Americans insist on driving on St. Croix like they do "back home," there will be chaos.

When it comes to marital, sexual, and family practices, are there right and wrong ways for society to function, or merely left and right options? The moral relativist would argue that there is no "wrong" as long as society flows smoothly. Yet those who believe in moral absolutes based on biblical revelation disagree. Traditional morality sees our culture on a collision course because we are choosing our own side of the road on which to drive, irrespective of traffic patterns. If, as Christianity contends, there is a divinely appointed way to live and practice, rejection of that way is cultural suicide. The good news is that there is still time and opportunity to turn things around.

Redeeming the Brave New Secular World

The specter of a world steeped in moral relativity is discomforting. However, despite the ethical decay that defines our present age, the future doesn't have to be a reenactment of Sodom and Gomorrah. There are ways to prevent the chaos from fully enveloping our age. The solution lies in the power of the gospel to enable society to change direction and in the willingness of Christians to speak and act in a way which models the divine intent for humanity.

If believers can exemplify the wisdom and benefit of a Bible-based morality, allowing Scripture to govern marriage, sexual practice, and values, then the watching world will see the contrast between secularism and Christianity. The world does not need a contrived "happiness" in which believers attempt to win others through trying to appear happier, holier, and more successful. The world needs what the church needs: an honest opportunity to experience the truth of God's plan for individuals, the family, and society.

If God's people would depend on God's plan, then the reality of what Christ offers would be apparent for all to see. Christians who maintain the positive values of Scripture constitute the thumb in the dike of immorality. While the threatening flood of chaos is held in abeyance, God continually works through believers to neutralize the danger. The choice is obvious: Either stand up and be counted among those who effectively testify to the saving and sustaining power of God, or else surrender and let cultural chaos prevail. Those who take the righteous stand can truly show a confused world how to find God in the chaos.

8

The Abandonment of Media

Who? What? Where? When? Why? How? These questions form the basic approach of the news-gathering media. But news reporting has become sophisticated. No longer does the public want reporting in the monotone style of the character Joe Friday in the television series "Dragnet" ("Just the facts, ma'am"). Instead, reporters often weave flair and commentary into news reports to make palatable what might otherwise be monotonous. Furthermore, every news reporter sees events through his or her own biases. Some reporters are more honest and careful in their attempts to remain objective, and many are unaware of the slant they give to the news.

It is quite clear that the content of the news today has been filtered through the values system of editors and reporters before it is seen in print, heard on the radio, or watched on television. In fact, not only are the particulars within a news story and the way they are presented subject to human judgment, but the question of whether even to *present* a news item must be decided. Without precise standards by which objectivity can be reasonably expected, and with the First Amendment to the U.S. Constitution protecting freedom of speech in America, one is left with choosing whether to trust or doubt media reports.

The abdication of media involvement by Christians does not portend a societal shift back to Christian values and assumptions. In fact, the simplest way to guarantee secular dominance is to allow the liberal media elite to continue calling the shots. If this occurs, any gains by the church in reaching the masses with the gospel will likely be downplayed, if reported at all. Replacing the positive impact of Christianity will be the caricatures and stereotyping that hold the Christian faith and its leadership up to ridicule and contempt.

In a country where some 50 percent of the people claim to be "born again," it is remarkable that so few are involved in the media. Whether by benign neglect or some grand design, the media members' wholesale rejection of Judeo-Christian values has become the drumbeat for society as it marches in lockstep toward secular humanism.

Conspiracy, or Unconscious Bias?

Media elite are not necessarily conspiring to undermine Christian values nor minimize the church's positive role in society. It's more a matter of secular media seeing things through their secular values. Most of the media players would not agree that an anti-Christian or liberal bias exists. However, their judgment is often clouded by secular assumptions which cannot relate to Christianity except in a negative way.

In 1988, for example, nationally syndicated radio and television broadcaster Larry King was a guest on my radio talk show. I asked him his opinion of what is often referred to as a "liberal bias" in the media. King was unwilling to concede without evidence that such a bias existed. Therefore, he put the burden on me to support the notion of bias by asking me, "For instance?" It so happened that just that same day, a front-page news item reported then-Vice-President George Bush's opposition to legislation called the "Civil Rights Restoration Act" (CRRA). The article led the unwary reader to think that by being against this bill, Bush was somehow against civil rights. No explanation was given as to why he was opposed to the bill, which happened to include his concern that the bill would be likely to force religious schools and even churches to hire people engaged in life-styles and practices abhorrent to Christianity. When I pointed this example out to Larry King, he remarked, "Yes, but that's just bad journalism." I told Larry (who happened to be in favor of the CRRA) that was my point. Whether intentionally misleading or sloppily reported, the net effect is the same: an inaccurate picture of the truth. Call it what you want, but the person wanting to know the news does not get objective, unbiased coverage.

Although the honest person would not want to replace a liberal media bias with a conservative one, more balance in media would be welcome. If more Christians broke into journalism and broadcast media, a parity could be achieved through offsetting biases. The challenge to the church is to recognize where the centers of influence are, beginning with media, and *occupy* (Luke 19:13—"to continue to do business") until the Lord returns. Obedience to this command is the key step in turning cultural surrender into Christian progress.

In a recent poll conducted by S. Robert Lichter, head of a Washington, D.C.-based organization that monitors the news media, the values and beliefs of elite media journalists were surveyed. These are the people from ABC, CBS, NBC, and PBS; national newspapers such as the *New York Times* and *Washington Post*; plus major news magazines such as *Time* and *Newsweek*.

A Gallup-type poll of a random sample of these journalists was taken. A certain homogeneity of the elitist broadcasters was apparent—they tended to be politically liberal and democratic, most coming from big cities in the Northeast. Specifically:

90% favor abortion rights
80% do not believe that homosexuality is wrong
47% find nothing wrong with adultery
80% support affirmative action for minorities
81% voted for liberal presidential candidate George McGovern
20% attend church or synagogue

These liberal views dominate news media, especially television news. It's as if the prerequisite for television journalism is an extreme liberal perspective on all social and political issues. In an article entitled "TV News: The Politics of Social Climbing," Dinesh D'Sousa wrote:

> No matter where he comes from . . . the aspiring TV journalist typically adopts a left-liberal world view as he picks up the tools of the trade. There is nothing conspirational in this. To get their stories on the air, TV journalists have to embrace the culture of network news, either consciously or unconsciously. . . . And since the culture of television journalism is liberal, it is hardly surprising that reporters get their idea of what is news—ultimately the most ideological question in journalism—from the whole range of left-liberal assumptions, inclinations and expectations.[1]

Just How Slanted Is the News?

The abortion issue is one of many areas of news reporting where bias is blatantly obvious. The coverage of the April 1989 National Organization for Women (NOW) march in Washington, D.C., compared with the "Rally for Life '90" gathering in Washington, D.C. in April of 1990 is eye-opening.

How many people attended these rallies? Various estimates say hundreds of thousands. But the attendance issue has been hotly debated, with plenty of indications that the pro-life crowd was significantly undercounted in news reports. There is no debate, however, over the manner in which these rallies were covered by media. First, consider the "balance" and "objectivity" of the print media:

— *USA Today* covered the NOW rally with numerous supportive articles, but barely mentioned the pro-life event.

— *Time* devoted a cover story and five pages of copy to the NOW march, but didn't include one word about the "Rally for Life '90."

— The *Washington Post* gave pre-rally publicity to the NOW rally in 1989, providing a map for the assistance of participants. The NOW event was proclaimed a triumph in a front-page, banner headline. There was also extensive post-march coverage. The "Rally for Life '90" was reported in the lower half of the page in the Metro section.

— *Newsweek*, as part of a lengthy coverage of the NOW rally, wrote:

> After years of losing the offensive in the bitter battle over abortion, a newly emboldened pro-choice movement was on the march again. Last week more than 300,000 demonstrators . . . surged through the streets of the capital to demonstrate their support for pro-choice.
>
> The turnout at the rally—one of the largest in the nation's history—far exceeded anybody's expectations. The organizers anticipated only 100,000 protestors. But as the busloads poured into Washington, it became apparent that a grassroots momentum had taken hold.[2]

Having provided this "unbiased" account of the abortion-rights rally of 1989, how did *Newsweek* cover the 1990 pro-life event? Actually, a better question is, "Did *Newsweek* cover the hundreds of thousands of pro-lifers who gathered in Washington, D.C., in April of 1990?" The answer is no— not one picture, not one word!

When media "report" controversial issues in such a manner, the not-so-subtle agenda is apparent: Advocacy and rhetoric are hidden by a thinly veiled disguise of "reporting" designed to sway the reader toward the point of view of the writer. In most other cases this would be called "propaganda," yet in issues such as abortion, this slanted coverage is palmed off as "objective journalism."

Whether one considers it refreshing or arrogant, some print media have actually admitted their bias. For example, in an editorial entitled "When Readers Are Wrong," the *Washington Post* wrote:

> The anti-abortion forces, for example, believe that The Post, institutionally, is "pro-choice." Of course it is. Any reader of the paper's editorials and home-grown columnists is aware of that. Moreover, while the shadings are more subtle, close textual analysis probably would reveal that, all things considered, our news coverage has favored the "pro-choice" side.[3]

Television journalists don't fare any better in their bias. Using the same example of comparing the 1989 pro-abortion and 1990 pro-life rallies, ABC called the NOW march "a great outpouring of sentiment" that "flooded the streets of Washington." The "Rally for Life '90" was called "a desperate act," implying the movement was on the decline. Cable News Network initially reported that only 60,000 had assembled for the pro-life rally. But even after revising their figures to 200,000 (due to outrage expressed by participants and observers), the coverage implied a disappointing turnout in light of the expectation of organizers.

Having seen that such an influential newspaper as the *Washington Post* admits its "pro-choice" bias, are other news media aware of and willing to admit their biases as well? In most cases they are not aware, so they will hardly fess-up to their lack of objectivity.

In an article on the question of whether a liberal bias exists in broadcast journalism, *New York Times* television critic John Corry stated, "There is no doubt this is so." But Corry insisted that the bias was unconscious and not deliberate. The blame didn't rest with the journalists, he contended, but with "the dominant culture," which he described as "the product of the opinions and preferences of America's artists and intellectuals."

According to Corry, this "dominant culture" supplies the moral dimension to his thinking, allowing him to identify goodness and just causes. The dominant culture is, in fact, the dominance of Corry's own liberal thinking and those of the left with whom he associates. It is ironic that such people view themselves as progressive, free thinkers, when in fact dissent from the liberal agenda is anathema.

An example of how liberals don't tolerate dissent in their ranks is their support of Martin Scorsese's *The Last Temptation of Christ*. Film critic Michael Medved, who panned the film, was asked why so many fellow critics came out in favor of such a boring, awful film. Medved said that he knew of several national film critics who admitted to him they also hated the film. But they felt constrained to support the film so as to avoid the appearance of supporting the likes of Jerry Falwell and Don Wildmon. So much for objectivity! Corry sums up this unwritten axiom of intolerant liberalism when he states, "The right wing is regarded as the enemy." This eye-opening summary should help conservatives in general and Christians in particular understand why they feel such hostility from secular media.

The *Los Angeles Times* Exposé

A breath of fresh air was felt in the summer of 1990 when the *Los Angeles Times* printed a four-part series on media bias. The specific focus of the series was the way in which the abortion issue was reported. The application, however, is much broader than the abortion controversy. Since the series clearly shows that reporters and editors intentionally slanted the news in favor of their own "pro-choice" point-of-view, then how can media be trusted to objectively report on anything of a controversial nature? Frankly, at this stage of the game they can't. Diogenes would have no success in finding his honest man in the offices of our leading newspapers, magazines, and television stations. Is this view a bit extreme, perhaps even cynical? Decide for yourself.

The *Los Angeles Times* series on "Abortion and the Media," written by David Shaw, appeared July 1-4, 1990. The series began by correctly stating that 80-90 percent of U.S. journalists, according to two major studies, personally favor abortion rights. Furthermore, the American Newspaper Guild—the union that represents the news and editorial employees at many major newspapers—has given its official endorsement to "freedom of choice in abortion decisions." The *Times* survey of how the press covers the abortion issue examined 18 months of major newspaper, television, and news magazine coverage. More than 100 interviews were conducted with journalists and with activists on both sides of the debate. Amid the insistence by pro-lifers that media bias is rampant, what did the investigation by the *Times* conclude? The comprehensive *Times* study "confirms that this bias often exists."

The *Times* series, while stating that "responsible journalists do try to be fair," demonstrates that there is a glut of irresponsible journalists in prominent places. The *Times* said, "Careful examination of stories published and broadcast reveals scores of examples, large and small, that can only be characterized as unfair to the opponents of abortion, either in content, tone, choice of language or prominence of play."[4]

The specific conclusions of the *Los Angeles Times* study on "Abortion and the Media" are:

- The news media consistently use language and images that frame the entire abortion debate in terms that implicitly favor abortion-rights advocates.

- Abortion-rights advocates are often quoted more frequently and characterized more favorably than are abortion opponents.

- Events and issues favorable to abortion opponents are sometimes ignored or given minimal attention by the media.

- Many news organizations have given more prominent play to stories on rallies or electoral and legislative victories by abortion-rights advocates than to stories on rallies and electoral and legislative victories by abortion rights opponents.

- Columns of commentary favoring abortion rights outnumber those opposing abortion by a margin of more than 2 to 1 on the opinion-editorial pages of most of the nation's major daily newspapers.

- Newspaper editorial writers and columnists alike, long sensitive to violations of First Amendment rights and other civil liberties in cases involving minority and anti-war protests, have largely ignored such questions when Operation Rescue and other abortion opponents have raised them.[5]

The Magnitude of Bias

Illustrations of bias in news-media reporting abound. A casual perusal of the television/radio dial or newspapers will reveal the slant away from a conservative position and toward the liberal view of moral life practices.

According to the *Times*, "coverage of abortion tends to be presented . . . from the abortion-rights perspective." For example, when the United States Supreme Court ruled in the case of *Webster v. Reproductive Health Services and Planned Parenthood* that states can have more latitude in regulating abortion, ABC News called the decision "a major setback for abortion rights," when it could just have easily been called "a major victory for the rights of the unborn."

Media have consistently reported on the abortion debate in ways which emphasize women, while consistently ignoring the unborn. The *Washington Post*, when writing about proposed pro-life legislation in Louisiana, spoke of the State House of Representatives making a decision on "a woman's reproductive rights." When the *Los Angeles Times* covered the same story, it referred to the proposed legislation as "the nation's harshest." From the abortion rights advocates' perspective, the legislation did involve a woman's reproductive rights and was "harsh." But pro-life advocates would view the legislation as dealing with the rights of the fetus and would describe it as "benevolent" toward the unborn.

Similarly, almost all media refer to anti-abortion legislation as "restrictive." What does it restrict? A woman's access to abortion. Why couldn't the legislation be referred to as "protective." What does it protect? The unborn baby. Media coverage clearly ignores this silent victim of abortion.

Further examples of bias include the way legislation regulating abortion is almost invariably described as "hurting poor women the most." The argument from abortion-rights advocates is that women of means will be able to travel to states where abortion is legal, while poor women are "hurt" by the inability to afford such travel. Why don't media ever say legislation regulating abortion would "help" the unborn babies of poor women by enabling them to be born? The *Times* concludes that the principal reason why legislation is never spoken of as "helping" the unborn is that media have accepted the abortion-rights view: There is no human life to be "helped" before birth.

When reporters make an honest effort to fairly describe both sides of the abortion debate, the bias of editors often enters the picture. Ethan Bonner, legal affairs reporter for the *Boston Globe*, had such an experience. In 1989 Bonner wrote a story for the *Globe* on late-term abortions. A copy editor took issue with Bonner's description of a surgical procedure "destroying" the unborn baby by "crushing forming skulls and bones." Bonner says he was told by the editor, "As far as I'm concerned, until that thing is born, it is really no different from a kidney; it is part of the woman's body." The editor said that to talk about "destroying" it or about "forming bones" is really to distort the issue. So much for objectivity and open-mindedness!

Skepticism, Yet Hope

The significance of the four-part *Los Angeles Times* series is that skepticism of media is not only warranted, it's a necessity. A society dominated by secularism and informed by a biased, secular media inevitably perpetuates chaos. Thus, it should be understood that attempts to direct people to a godly path through the confusion and chaos will likely be misperceived. The pro-life community has been substantially vindicated from accusations that it is paranoid and hypercritical of media reporting. However, Christians need to continue to persevere, despite popular sentiments which are easily manipulated by secular forces. While the church ought to constantly monitor the media for fairness, she should also encourage believers to occupy the prominent places within media so as to assure more balance and objectivity. By actively assuming such important roles, Christians could renew their hope of a level playing field and the logical consequences of reemerging as a dominant force in our culture.

9

Activism:
The Last Temptation of Christ

It is clear from the New Testament that the focus of the church includes evangelism and discipleship (Matthew 28:19,20). Believers are to be strengthened in their faith through teaching, worship, and opportunities for service. New believers are to be added through the presentation of the gospel. But is the mission of the church limited to preaching the gospel and teaching the saints? Many will answer "yes" to this question, contending that man's greatest need is for eternal life through faith in Christ.

Any effort to change society through involvement in social issues is seen by many believers as a sidetrack, diverting Christians from their mission of presenting eternal solutions to that of fixing temporal problems. Often accompanying this view is a type of cultural pessimism which sees society as inevitably getting worse and worse. Therefore, the rhetoric says, "Why polish the brass on a sinking ship?" If the world is sinking into a sea of judgment, then isn't the most important task to point people to the lifeboats before it's too late?

A problem inherent in the view that evangelism and discipleship constitute the exclusive mission of the church is that this position presents a false "either/or" dichotomy. Must it be evangelism or activism? Are we limited to discipleship or social involvement? Why not evangelism, discipleship, and cultural activism? If these concerns are properly balanced, there will be both the prominent assertion of Christ as the solution to eternal needs, and presentation of the Bible as a guide to solutions for temporal, societal needs.

There is a potential problem in leaning too far toward social and political involvement. Many denominations have slowly succumbed to preaching social concerns, while ignoring both the spiritual roots of social problems and the eternal consequences which result from rebelling against God. This "social gospel" is commendable for its work of charity and benevolence, but is contemptible for its neglect of eternal issues.

An exclusively social gospel which neglects the eternal is like a rattlesnake bite. The venom from the rattlesnake contains a good deal of protein, which is healthy and beneficial to the victim of a bite. However, the toxins in the venom do major damage to the vascular and neurological systems of the body, often leading to death. Therefore any positive benefit of a rattlesnake bite is outweighed by its mortal threat. Similarly, a social gospel contains "protein" as in the snake bite. It has some benefit to society: helping people in need, feeding the hungry, making the world a better place in which to live. But without an eternal hope the recipients of social assistance die spiritually from the toxin of sin—a poison which is not overcome by the meeting of social needs.

A Theology of Pessimism or Cultural Involvement

Without regard to the soundness of particular beliefs, it must be recognized that beliefs themselves will determine how one sees the present role of Christians in society. This is especially true in relation to one's view of the return of Christ. For those who hold the belief that the return of Christ is imminent, certain applications to the mission of the church logically follow. For instance, during World War II one particular Christian institution on the West Coast is said to have carefully considered whether low cost, inferior plumbing materials should be used in the construction of new buildings instead of expensive, long-lasting materials. At the time, there were many who strongly believed that the Italian fascist leader, Benito Mussolini, was the Antichrist, whose presence signified the immediate return of Christ to earth.

The issue was whether the more costly plumbing materials could be justified in light of the limited use period before the Lord returned. It was argued that the money could be better spent On efforts to reach the unbeliever before it was too late. Fortunately, having no guarantee that Mussolini was the Antichrist, the school decided to opt for the longer-lasting materials—a decision which, in hindsight, continues to bring relief to the school's leaders!

Examples such as the case of the Christian school mentioned above are numerous. Most readers are aware of well-intentioned individuals whose view of prophecy convinced them to abandon future plans of education, training, or career planning in order to take to the streets and preach, in anticipation of the imminent return of Christ. Although the caricature of an odd-looking fellow carrying a sandwich board sign proclaiming, "Repent! The end of the world is near!" is not very realistic, the attitude expressed by such a cartoon image is real. And the notion that civilization is a sinking ship about to go under in judgment justifies for many the urgency of the church focusing solely on pointing the way to the lifeboats.

If the position which holds that apostasy—not revival—will precede Christ's return is correct, what difference should it make in the mission and methods of the church? Should there not still be evangelistic fervor, zeal for discipling believers, and a desire to make the world a better place until God Himself brings down the curtain? The belief that the last days will be characterized by apostasy is based on a legitimate interpretation of the biblical data, whether right or wrong. But the application of this belief should not, and must not, be used to justify nor excuse failure of the church to impact society.

If one's view of the last days causes a cultural retreat, the net effect upon the culture will be similar to what might have happened during World War II had Christians acted upon the commonly held belief that Mussolini was the Antichrist. If Christian schools opted for cheap plumbing materials in constructing buildings due to the belief that the end was imminent, there would eventually have been severe consequences. To accept the notion that the church is doomed to fail in her efforts at penetrating secular culture with the Christian message will likewise create severe negative consequences. These consequences include cultural abandonment by believers and justification for the dismal evangelistic results which are consistent with cultural retreat.

There's an old adage regarding how the Christian life ought to be lived in view of the imminent return of Christ. It says to be ready as if Christ were coming back today, but to make plans as if He weren't returning for another thousand years. This seems to be a sensible approach for the vast number of premillennial Christians: living in holy expectancy of Christ's imminent return, but committed to working for the duration of what could be a protracted campaign.

Lest the church find herself building with inferior materials, belief in an imminent return should not affect the short- and long-term plans for reaching the world for Christ. Without a divine guarantee concerning the time of Christ's return (which the Bible says only the Father knows—Matthew 24:36), allowing a prophetic interpretation to hinder the program of the church is subtly to work against the gospel itself. Therefore, nothing inherent in a premillennial view of Christ's return prevents both evangelistic efforts aimed at individuals and cultural evangelism aimed at heightening the impact of Christianity upon the world at large.

Alternatives and Making Repairs

If inevitable apostasy characterizes the days preceding Christ's return, then in a devious sort of way Christians could rejoice when things become worse. This parallels Romans 6:1,2 where the apostle Paul asks, "Are we to continue in sin that grace might increase? May it never be!" To welcome apostasy and cultural decay because they might prophetically portend an imminent return of Christ is an abomination. The misguided expediency of such a view is the antithesis of biblical Christianity. Not only can this line of reasoning be seen as sordidly accepting the horror of a Third Reich, but those who seek to prevent another Holocaust could be accused of frustrating the will of God!

Another view of prophecy is often criticized for its insistence that the dominion of the church in society will usher in the return of Christ, so therefore Christians should try to have an impact upon culture in fulfillment of God's plan. Contrast this with a belief that apostasy and cultural decay will usher in the return of Christ, so therefore Christians should abandon culture in order to facilitate God's "plan." Since no one has a pipeline to eternity which resolves the question of the correct millennial view, isn't the best course for the church one which desires the greatest impact and influence of Christianity upon individuals and society? Peace rather than war. Love rather than hate. Morality rather than immorality. Increasing the visibility of the Christian message rather than suppressing it. Belief rather than skepticism. Biblical humanism instead of secular humanism. Praying for revival instead of praying for apostasy. Perilous times and great tribulation will arrive soon enough. It is the church's privilege and responsibility to resist the takeover of darkness by letting the light shine.

Whether this world has a long time or a short time before Christ returns, there is a simple approach for the church that balances evangelism with cultural involvement. While explaining the proper use of the lifeboats, why not make necessary repairs to the ship to keep it afloat? Perhaps Christianity can (and should) prevent the sinking of culture into the depths of depravity. With some believers taking the helm while others plug up the leaks, the ship of civilization can be given both direction and stability.

By infiltrating areas such as law, education, media, and the arts, Christianity can regain its former prominence as a faith worth espousing and a worldview worth considering. The essence of Christianity cannot be successfully misconstrued when there are sufficient numbers of Christians serving as watchmen on the walls. With informed believers ready, willing, and able to correct false notions about the faith, occupying positions of influence within society provides a means for believers to attest to the truth. Jesus said His disciples are "the salt of the earth" and "the light of the world" (Matthew 5:13,14). Just as salt preserves through penetrating food, and light illuminates by penetrating darkness, so believers can preserve and illuminate society by penetrating and infiltrating it at all levels.

> How shall they believe in Him whom they
> have not heard? And how shall they hear without
> a preacher? And how shall they preach unless
> they are sent? (Romans 10:14,15).

Christians have been sent to proclaim and live the gospel. Believers are called to be the proclaimers of the good news and the preservers of godliness. It is a myopic view of the mission of the church which sees evangelism as a task performed by professional clergy within the church service. Instead, all believers have been sent to be witnesses of the saving grace of God and the biblical blueprint for living. This mission is accomplished where the greatest needs exist: before individuals and a society which dwell in darkness. The challenge for the church is to turn from inward isolation and break down the barriers which keep Christianity from engaging culture and occupying prominent positions of influence within society. Rather than retreat, it is time to advance, returning to the long-neglected biblical pattern of personal and cultural evangelism.

Activism in Action

In February of 1988 rumors circulated about a motion picture being made which allegedly depicted Jesus Christ in a blatantly false, offensive way. The film was said to be based on a novel by the late neo-pagan writer Nikos Kazantzakis. By spring 1988 the rumors proved to be true, setting off an international debate and an avalanche of protest.

Kazantzakis had previously written in his book *Saviors of God*, "It is not God who will save us—it is we who will save God, by battling, by creating and transmuting matter into spirit."[1] In Greek author Kazantzakis' fictionalized account of Jesus entitled *The Last Temptation of Christ*, Jesus is portrayed as a confused, bewildered, and lust-driven man, who fantasizes about making love to Mary Magdalene while hanging on the cross. The Jesus of Kazantzakis is a wimpish sinner whose own mother, Mary, believes is crazy.

Given the fact that belief in nothing has become endemic in Hollywood, it was just a matter of time before someone attempted to put the ranting of Kazantzakis (for which he was excommunicated and refused burial in his native Greece by the Greek Orthodox Church) on film. There was precedent for "daring" producers to exploit the popularity of Jesus by presenting Him in a negative light—a move virtually guaranteed to evoke some reaction. For example, a Scandinavian "film producer" depicted Jesus as a homosexual in the early 1980s.

But the story of *The Last Temptation of Christ* was destined to be different. The film project, originally dropped by Paramount Pictures in 1983, had been revived by one of the largest film companies in the world: Universal Pictures. As if that alone wasn't sufficient for an epic battle over religious insensitivity versus artistic license, the director of the film was Martin Scorsese. Scorsese's previous projects included *Taxi Driver* and *Raging Bull*—films which dealt with the dark and sinister side of life and of the characters portrayed. The combination of Universal Pictures (owned by the entertainment giant MCA) and Scorsese set the stage for the greatest uproar in the history of filmmaking, and an opportunity for hundreds of thousands of Christians to become "activists."

Drawing the Battle Lines

Jesus admonished His followers to "go therefore and make disciples of all the nations" (Matthew 28:19). St. Paul wrote to Jude regarding the need to "contend earnestly for the faith which was once for all delivered to the saints" (Jude 3). The "great commission" for believers includes "contending earnestly for the faith." When the gospel of Christ is distorted, whether through misrepresenting who Christ is or what He did, it is incumbent upon believers to correct such distortions. The greater the distortion, the greater the need for outspoken correction and clarification. No one, however, could have anticipated how widespread the distortion of the Person of Christ would be through *The Last Temptation of Christ* film. But neither could anyone have predicted how far-reaching the opportunity was to present the truth about Christ, in response to the distortions raised by the film.

As rumors about the *Last Temptation* film continued to grow, it was becoming more apparent each day that the controversy was not going to go away. In April of 1988 I interviewed Tim Penland, a media consultant and evangelical Christian, who had been hired by Universal Pictures to build bridges between the Christian community and the film company's *Last Temptation* project. Penland, who subsequently determined he was being used by Universal to allay the legitimate concerns of Christians, was led to believe that the film was going to be "faith-affirming." He attempted to disarm objections to the film by presenting

Universal's promises to him that Christian leaders would have an opportunity to preview the film in plenty of time before its scheduled release in late September 1988. What could be fairer?

The statements by Penland that the film would be "faith-affirming" (an assurance made by Scorsese to Universal and relayed to Penland) and that Christian leaders would preview the film before public release held in abeyance the mounting concern. However, many people continued to be skeptical—especially those who were becoming knowledgeable about the content of the Kazantzakis novel behind the film. I queried whether such an unmitigated piece of sordid mischaracterization as Kazantzakis' book could be adapted to film in a way acceptable to Christians. The screenwriters would have to rewrite the entire book. It was as if a well-known director claimed to be making a film based on *Mein Kampf* which would be uplifting to Jews. The more I thought about it and discussed it with my radio audience, the more preposterous the notion became: A film by a secular film company, headed by non-Christians, directed by a nominal Roman Catholic, based on a heretical book by an excommunicated neo-paganist was supposed to be faith-affirming! It was time to act.

An Avalanche of Response

In May and early June of 1988 we regularly discussed the implications of the *Last Temptation* film on my program and considered how best to respond. In many cases it would be irresponsible to give substantial airtime to issues which would be forgotten by the next day. But in certain cases it would be irresponsible not to sufficiently cover issues which have far-reaching and long-lasting consequences. The *Last Temptation of Christ* controversy was such an issue.

From numerous discussions and updates, we were able to obtain names and phone numbers for some of the responsible parties at Universal Pictures. The calls began to trickle into Universal, then began to flood their switchboard with pleas not to defame or misrepresent Jesus Christ. Other people wrote letters, and still others circulated petitions, calling on Universal to stop the release of the film or else suffer the consequences of offending millions of people. Meanwhile, the media began picking up on the story and began the first of what became a monotonous, overused, and unfair depiction of protestors as people who were upset "by a film they hadn't even seen."

For hundreds and hundreds of people (eventually becoming hundreds of thousands), their first involvement in activism through phone calls, letters, and petitions was contemptuously misconstrued and demeaned in the secular media. Unpleasant but necessary lessons were learned about the impact of media on stories and the need to expect opposition whenever a stand is taken for what appears to be right. The media would be responsible for shifting attention off the scandalous content of the Kazantzakis book, the script, and the film by constantly condensing the entire controversy down to three allegations, each of them leveled at the film's protestors: "They haven't seen the film they're criticizing, they are acting as self-appointed censors, and they are anti-semitic."

Despite false depictions in the media about concerns over *The Last Temptation*, the protests against the film continued to grow by leaps and bounds. Universal Pictures had thrown down the gauntlet, and Christians across the world had picked it up. Universal continued its attempts to prop up the film, including a screening of the film for a "select group" of religious leaders in New York on July 12. These "leaders" were a handpicked group of mostly liberal clergy who could be counted on to give rave reviews of the film, which they did.

Meanwhile, Christian leaders in southern California formally announced their opposition to the film at a news conference held on July 12. These leaders, including Jack Hayford, Lloyd Ogilvie, Bill Bright, and James Dobson (who was unable to attend the conference), had given the film and Universal Pictures every possible benefit of the doubt. But the duplicitous actions of MCA/Universal were by this point undeniable. The inside story of Universal's dealings had been laid out for them by Tim Penland and his associate Larry Poland, who had come to realize both the insincerity of Universal and the need to publicly expose the scandalous film.

Since I had become somewhat visible in my opposition to *The Last Temptation of Christ*, I began receiving invitations to debate the issues surrounding the film. One such opportunity was on KABC radio, the Los Angeles affiliate of the ABC radio network. My opponent was the Rev. Charles Bergstrom, chairman of People for the American Way's executive committee. People for the American Way is a leftist organization founded by television producer Norman Lear. Its mission seems to be playing the counterpart to the now-defunct Moral Majority of Jerry Falwell. In the dialogue I had with Rev. Bergstrom, it was clear that the "beautiful people" of Hollywood's left felt that a fictionalized account of Jesus, no matter how controversial or offensive, was the type of film people needed to see. Not only was nothing sacred in Hollywood any longer, but there seemed to be an enjoyment of "religion bashing" under the guise of artistic exploration.

After the July 12 news conference by the Christian leaders, I began to pull out all stops in my denunciation of *The Last Temptation*. Besides the Kazantzakis novel there was now testimony from those who had been at the July 12 New York screening that the film was actually worse than previously anticipated! With novel, script, screenplay, and eyewitness testimony of the film available, any jury in the world would have come to the conclusion that *The Last Temptation* was an insensitive, false, and offensive portrayal of the Man worshiped as Lord and God by hundreds of millions of people worldwide.

The option of ignoring *The Last Temptation* was long gone by the middle of July. Being relatively inexperienced at demonstrating and protesting, I was unsure of the most effective way to tell the world that the Jesus of the Bible was exceedingly different than the Jesus of Kazantzakis/Universal. Besides the phone calls, letters, and petitions, I knew that there must be more which could be done. On Monday, July 18, I received a call while on the air from a man who was already planning to bring a group of protestors to Universal Studios in Universal City—which also happened to be the site of Universal Pictures' parent company, MCA. The man—John Frattarola from Calvary Chapel in West Covina—had organized a few busloads of people to show up on Wednesday, July 20.

I wanted to find out more about John's plans, so I spoke with him after the show. He and his fellow organizer, Peter Claproth, asked me to lead the protest and handle the media. I was glad to accept the challenge and announced the protest on my show the next day. It seemed fitting for me to take a prominent role in the demonstration since the MCA/Universal complex is a mere two miles down Lankershim Boulevard from my radio station, KKLA, in North Hollywood. The beast was in our backyard, and it was time to take action.

Putting Feet to the Protest

I announced the demonstration on Wednesday—the day before the event. I had no idea how many people would show up at noon on a weekday with less than 24 hours' notice. When Thursday arrived I was apprehensive yet confident that "all things work together for good" (Romans 8:28). As I arrived approximately 20 minutes before the scheduled start of the protest, dozens and dozens of people had already gathered, many of them carrying signs denouncing the film and promoting the Jesus of the Bible. Our gathering place was in front of MCA's world headquarters—a black monolith down the hill and around the corner from Universal Studios.

Upon my arrival I noticed that television camera crews were also arriving, and there were numerous police at the scene. I was immediately called over to speak with a field commander from North Hollywood Police, who wanted to know our intentions. I assured him we intended to lawfully and peaceably assemble, march to the entrance of Universal Studios, and return. I noted what was obvious from a glance at the growing crowd: The protestors were the bedrock of the communities, family people, mothers with babies, folks who had taken time off work to let their voices be heard. In contrast to the often-violent antiwar protests of the '60s, this group rather than being anti-establishment consisted of committed Christians who were pro-establishment, pro-police, pro-law and order, and pro-decency. The closest thing to the antiestablishment radicals of the '60s were the people at Universal/MCA who were challenging the very roots of Christianity by their production of *The Last Temptation*.

I addressed the media who had gathered in the midst of the throng of demonstrators. It wasn't difficult to anticipate most of their questions, such as "How can you protest a film you haven't seen?" I noted that the novel, script, screenplay, and eyewitnesses of the film provided plenty of evidence to render a verdict. A jury doesn't actually see a crime committed, but hears testimony regarding the allegations that a crime was committed, and on that basis determines guilt or innocence.

There was a tinge of disappointment in the faces of some of the reporters who had expected the protestors to be half-baked, anti-semitic, bigoted censors, whose narrow-mindedness they figured was confirmed by prematurely condemning a film yet to be seen. I thanked the Lord that my comments, which made the national news, were more indicative of the true nature of the demonstrators: people who were concerned that the film's distortion of Jesus would prevent others from finding the love and forgiveness they had experienced through Him. It wasn't insecurity with their own faith that brought people out. A film cannot change history. But a film such as *The Last Temptation* can present a historical person such as Jesus in such a repugnant way that those lacking a personal relationship with Him might be repelled from seeking to know the real Jesus.

When I had concluded my remarks to the press, I looked around and saw that I was surrounded by hundreds and hundreds of demonstrators—more than 2000 people! We proceeded to march down Lankershim and up the hill, with hundreds of signs telling our story to passersby. I was accompanied at the front of the march by Irv Rubin, head of the Jewish Defense League, whose presence made it clear that despite the fact that the corporate heads of MCA and Universal were Jewish, the issue was not "Christian versus Jews." In fact, Irv said that in his opinion Lew Wasserman, chairman of MCA, was "about as Jewish as the pope." Funny how so many in the media, whether intentional or otherwise, never clarified the "anti-semitic" issue they had raised.

When approximately 2500 people take to the streets on a weekday afternoon, most of them showing up on less than 24 hours' notice, the outpouring of concern can only be described as awesome. Probably 99 percent of the people who took part in the protest were demonstrating for the first time in their lives. The remarks I began hearing from the marchers were consistent: Their participation was one of the most significant events in their lives. The shift from passivity and cursing the darkness to activism was a transformation.

What Do You Do for an Encore?—An Epic Event!

Our July 20 rally and protest with some 2500 people attending was perhaps the largest demonstration against a film in Hollywood's history. Word of the nature and success of the protest spread quickly as participants shared their feelings of satisfaction that they had done something to make a difference. I discussed with my brother Don and with the organizers from Calvary Chapel West Covina the possibility of another protest march.

Rather than having peaked, the feelings about the film were continuing to build, and many people who missed the chance to march on July 20 wanted to make their own statement.

After consulting with the protest strategists, we determined that another rally was not only appropriate but necessary. I checked my schedule and wanted to set up the next protest at least two weeks ahead. Because of an out-of-state speaking engagement, I told the others that the second week in August was the best time for me, which gave us three weeks to organize the event from scratch. I decided that a Thursday would be the best day for the rally, since the chance for television coverage and viewing would be greater than on a weekend. We wanted the world to see our unity in standing for the Jesus of history. The others agreed with me. Thursday, August 11, 1988, was a day destined to be remembered.

Hollywood is the place where blockbuster films are planned. Unfortunately, many of the motion pictures which are promoted as "epic" end up being forgettable failures. But since Hollywood understands razzle and dazzle and since the film and television industries play the "number game" in terms of box office receipts and ratings, our protest would have to be of such proportions that no one could ignore the message we were sending. Although we ran the risk of being presumptuous about the anticipated size of our upcoming protest, we believed that the desired impact demanded a large turnout. Would as many as 10,000 people join us on a Thursday afternoon? We attempted to set our sights high.

The week following our first protest march I decided to call Rev. Don Wildmon, head of the American Family Association (AFA) in Tupelo, Mississippi. Although Tupelo is far removed from Hollywood in terms of values as well as geographically, the AFA had been at the forefront of *The Last Temptation* controversy from the beginning. When I reached Don Wildmon, he indicated that he was about to call me. He had heard of our July 20 protest and wanted to join forces. Don had spearheaded an antipornography rally previously which had attracted some 10,000 protestors and was anxious to have at least that many, if not more, show up for a protest of *The Last Temptation.*

As Don and I talked, I immediately sensed a man deeply committed to Christian activism. But unlike other well-known Christian leaders, Don was willing to use his resources to help make the protest a success without being the quarterback. His selflessness and servant's heart have enabled him to make major impacts in protecting and defending Christian values.

Don suggested a Sunday rally, which would give people a chance to participate after church. I told him my reasons for wanting a weekday demonstration. After hearing me, he agreed that a Thursday noon rally would be best. He agreed to play whatever role in the rally I and the organizers saw fit, and we both went to work planning the event.

Many people assisted in the planning of the August 11 rally. Details such as traffic control, a sound system, crowd control, and logistics were discussed. One question we faced was Where do 10,000 people go after they march? The front lawn of the MCA world headquarters was barely able to accommodate the 2500 or so we had at the July 20 protest, so that was out. Finally we discovered the existence of a park just two blocks from MCA headquarters, which would be ideal for a gathering.

Our plan was to have an 11:00 A.M. news conference on the day of the event at the main entrance to Universal Studios. Then at noon we would march down the hill and over to the park—a distance of barely more than a mile. I heavily promoted the rally on my daily broadcast, encouraging people to bring their signs and join the throngs in a positive demonstration of unity.

For the news conference I chose a wide cross section of the religious community to address the reporters at the news conference. Most of those invited were able to attend. The actual participants in the news conference included Bill Bright, founder of Campus Crusade for Christ; Rich Buehler, radio talk show host; Jane Chastain, broadcaster and board member of Concerned Women for America; Rosey Grier, former football great, actor, and head of an inner-city ministry; Paul Crouch, president of Trinity Broadcasting Network; Ken Wales, motion picture producer and director; Don Wildmon, founder of the American Family Association; Steve Gooden, recording artist; Dennis Prager, radio personality; Haim Asa, rabbi; and myself.

As meetings continued and further plans were laid out for the August 11 rally, new opportunities arose for contrasting the Jesus of the Bible with the Jesus of *The Last Temptation*. I was interviewed by *People* magazine, the *Washington Post*, and several other newspapers and publications. Although many of the various news media interviews seemed somewhat fair, an outstanding example of even-handed, balanced journalism was MacNeil-Lehrer's Geoffrey Boyd. Talking to the press is similar to rolling dice. The outcome is uncertain, but you hope for the best and do your homework so as to be ready to intelligently answer questions that arise. When people asked about all the free publicity our protests were giving to *The Last Temptation* film, I responded by recounting all the opportunities I and others had to tell people who Jesus really is. It's not often that national publications such as *People* magazine call me up and ask, "Who is Jesus Christ?" It was my privilege to tell them.

Activism was put in high gear during the last week of July. Since I was speaking at a Christian camp in Auburn, Washington, the first week of August, faithful and capable people were continuing to organize and refine the details for the rally in my absence. Even though Universal Pictures had set a release date for the film of September 23, the interest in taking a stand against the film had reached the boiling point by the first week of August.

In a conference call to protest organizers on August 3, spirits were high as the particulars began to fall in place for the August 11 event. There was a sense of divine destiny accompanying our righteous indignation. We had a cause and a legitimate purpose for wanting to be heard. Little did we know that events beyond our control would play into the hands of our protest.

Divine Providence? You Bet!

The day after our August 3 conference call, I received shocking news: Universal, attempting to capitalize on the flood of controversy, decided to change the release date of *The Last Temptation of Christ*. Instead of September 23, they moved the release up 43 days to August 12! Since we had been planning our August 11 protest for more than two weeks, it was providential that now our rally would take place on the eve of the release of the film. Coincidence or divine appointment?

The multitudes began descending upon the focal point of the upheaval over *The Last Temptation* film: Universal Studios. At 10:00 A.M. I met with the news conference participants at the KKLA studios in North Hollywood, two miles up the street from the site of the protest. After committing the rally to the Lord in prayer, we made an unforgettable journey down Lankershim Boulevard. Everywhere we looked there were people walking toward the site of the news conference and rally and up the hill to the entrance of Universal Studios. As I rode to the site with Rosey Grier, I remarked how the whole controversy had been a blessing in disguise since the day marked the end of apathy and the beginning of activism for thousands of Christians.

By the time we arrived at the scene of the news conference, more than 5000 people had already gathered, and the time of our protest march was still more than an hour away. The media had their cameras set in a semicircle, with the conference participants seated in front of the fountain at the entrance to Universal Studios. There were at least a dozen microphones on the lectern we had set up, and the whole place buzzed with excitement. For the curious tourists who happened to choose that day to take the Universal Studios Tour, they certainly got more entertainment than they bargained for. Helicopters buzzed overhead, mounted police stood by, and thousands of singing, sign-carrying Christians radiated a righteous countenance that shone as bright as the August sun.

The news conference almost seemed surreal. I began the conference by reading an open letter to MCA/Universal denouncing the film. One of the highlights of the news conference was when Steve Gooden, a handsome, young black singer, displayed his recording contract with MCA Records, a subsidiary of MCA. Steve relayed his concern about *The Last Temptation* and challenged others to "stand for a righteous cause—to put convictions for Christ ahead of their own personal gain." Having said that, Steve began ripping his contract to pieces, proclaiming, "I tear this contract in the name of my Lord Jesus Christ." Tears. Applause. A standing ovation. No script could have better created the drama of the real-life decision of Steve Gooden to put the truth above consequences.

By the time our news conference had finished, it was nearly noon. The crowd had swelled to enormous proportions, with more people arriving by the minute. Those still on their way to the protest created a massive traffic jam on the Hollywood freeway, estimated by reporters to be a 14-mile backup. Streets were sealed off by police as gridlock set in. Late arrivers had to park up to two miles away. Even though we knew that literally thousands of people were still on the way, the restless crowd wanted to march.

At just a few minutes after noon, we headed down the hill from the entrance to Universal Studios toward Lankershim. Those who were participants in the news conference led the way. The countless thousands of activist Christians chanted, "Boycott MCA" and sang hymns. It was not easy keeping a slow marching pace down the steep, winding hill, so we had to stop several times to keep the group at a safe speed. As I turned to look up the hill at the following crowd, I thought how we looked like the Roman legions marching to victory.

When we were first planning the march I had enquired about a parade permit. I found out that we needed to apply at least 30 days before an event in order to receive a permit. As we turned right at the bottom of the hill onto Lankershim, it became clear that we had commandeered the streets. Lankershim had been closed to traffic, and the police did a wonderful job in accommodating us. Whether we needed a parade permit or not became academic. The largest demonstration in the history of Hollywood was authorized by a higher power!

As we assembled in the park for singing and testimony, the magnitude of the event became even clearer. Resolute, determined believers had made a sacrifice: men and women taking time from work to participate, mothers with infants in strollers, pushing along their children; high school and college students who could have been at the beach, holding signs and making their statements; senior citizens who braved the August heat to gather and march for the Jesus of history. People of all shapes, sizes, colors, ages, and religious affiliations came—people by the thousands. The captain of the North Hollywood Police Department later estimated the crowd to be a minimum of 25,000, with separate estimates that the traffic jam we created prevented thousands more from ever arriving at the rally.

Involvement: the Life-Blood of Activism

As we concluded the rally in the park with the singing of "God Bless America," people began heading back to their various responsibilities. During the same week the same scene, only on a smaller scale, was played out in other locations across the country. I continue to hear people refer to the August 11 rally as not only one of the most memorable, significant days of their lives but also the beginning of their active involvement in issues affecting Christianity. In one fell swoop 25,000 activists were recruited into God's army.

The future of Christian activism is dependent on the willingness of believers to get involved so as to make a difference in society. If someone takes a junker car—rusted out, with no wheels—and dumps it on your street, you might object to the eyesore. If the same car were left across the street from your home, there's a greater chance that you'd take action. If the car ended up in front of your own house, then most people would take steps to get it removed. And if the junker blocked your own driveway, you would definitely take action to correct the problem. The question, is How close to home do things have to get before you take action to correct the problem?

The August 11 rally stands as an example of unity, commitment, and involvement. The desire is resident in the believer. The challenge is to take the flame that flickers within and fan it into a raging fire. If the church can unleash the zeal within believers, both individual lives and society as a whole can be transformed through the power of the Jesus Christ of history. Activism is not an option. It's a biblically mandated involvement in society as believers fulfill their role of being salt and light.

A final perspective is to see the biblical calling to servanthood as a calling to activism—for what is servanthood, if not the active meeting of needs by God's people? If activism is understood in this light—taking a visible stand for Jesus at every level of society, bringing biblical answers to the dilemmas our age faces—then we can better appreciate a simple paraphrase of the words of Christ: "Well done, good and faithful activist. Enter into the joy of your Lord" (Matthew 25:21).

10

The Polarizing Effect of the Pro-Life Movement

Both in America and around the world the issue of abortion has divided families, churches, communities, and even nations. The importance of the issue itself, together with its effect on Christianity, makes the abortion question one which must be fully understood. The problem is that few believers have taken the time to learn the issues of the abortion debate, leaving the pro-life movement short on strategy and sound arguments although long on zeal and emotional involvement. Since the abortion controversy has the potential of polarizing the church as a whole, it is vital to come to grips with a strategy which doesn't restrain Christianity's impact upon society.

The biblical teaching that human beings have been created in the image of God (Genesis 1:27) is the foundation for the concept of the sanctity of human life. Although there is disagreement among biblical scholars regarding the meaning of the "image of God," the consensus is that this refers to a moral and spiritual image. Humans have been created with a special dignity as well as the capacity to desire to know and worship God. Furthermore, mankind is able to make moral choices. The law of the jungle and the laws of civilization are diametrically opposed.

Although the abortion debate within society is not properly a religious debate, there are religious aspects. For example, the fact that humans are created in the image of God (Genesis 1:27) and the numerous biblical references to a special recognition and calling of people before they were born (Jeremiah 1:5, Luke 1:44, Galatians 1:15), reinforce a religious duty to promote and protect the sanctity of life before and after birth. As such, authentic Christianity cannot sit by passively in the debate over the unborn. Nor should anyone who accepts Scripture as a basis of faith and practice be indifferent toward the hundreds of thousands of abortions performed in the United States alone every year. But where does a person begin in order to change the way society allows the unborn to be treated?

A Method to the Madness

That life is precious and worthy of protection is axiomatic, even among virtually all secularists. In a quasi-theological sense this equates to the biblical notion of the sanctity of life. Notwithstanding a general agreement in society regarding the specialness of human life, the debate over abortion continues. The main reason that "pro-life" and "pro-choice" groups rarely seem to agree is that the focus of the respective positions is different. The "pro-life" view emphasizes the need to recognize and protect the rights of the unborn. The "pro-choice" view emphasizes the need for women to maintain control over their own reproduction without outside interference. Thus the debate is similar to a sporting event where the teams show up at two different stadiums. Pro-life fights the battle in the arena of the unborn, pro-choice in the arena of women. Despite the difference in emphasis, there is common ground and there are ways to argue on behalf of the unborn without alienating people from Christianity. For positive changes to occur, there must be an understanding of the effect of changing laws as compared to the effect of changing society's attitude about abortion.

Laws regarding abortion have run the gamut from total protection for the unborn to no protection whatsoever. Presently, laws are quite liberal in permitting the pregnant woman alone the decision of whether or not to abort. The biological father of the unborn baby and the fetus itself are usually granted no rights or minimal rights, respectively. As a result, in the United States pro-life advocates have tried since 1973 to overturn the landmark abortion decision of *Roe v. Wade*, which essentially provides for abortion on demand (for any reason or no reason).

Although a change in laws regarding abortion would afford more protection for the unborn and result in fewer abortions, the typical pro-life reliance on a legal solution to the abortion problem is insufficient. It is not only the laws which need changing but also society's attitude toward abortion and sexuality. An antiwar slogan of the Vietnam era asked, "Suppose they gave a war and nobody came?" The point was that even with a declaration of war, if people refused to participate, no war would take place. Likewise, suppose there were abortion clinics but no one entered? Even if abortion remained legal, no abortions would take place.

The present challenge is to convince women and men of the wrongfulness of killing the unborn and to promote alternatives to abortion and responsible sexuality. Without such a change in attitude relative to abortion, even if laws were changed to make abortion illegal (as was the case in most states before 1973), illegal abortions would simply take the place of legal ones. But the holocaust of abortion can be stopped even without the help of the law if society's attitude about abortion changes. However, even with the law on the side of the unborn, society must change its thinking for abortion to cease.

Since most of the energy of the pro-life movement within the church has been spent on changing laws, there must be a reorientation toward changing the way people think about abortion. In order to be successful in this endeavor, certain practices must cease and others, which have been neglected, must begin. For some, this means reassessing pro-life strategy. For most, it means developing a strategy. A biblically balanced strategy must also avoid hindering the impact of the Christian gospel upon society in the quest to protect the unborn. Current pro-life efforts are often close to following in the footsteps of Pyrrhus, king of Epirus. His military strategy enabled him to win battles over the Romans in 280 and 279 B.C. However, his losses were so heavy that he lost the war and his empire. Winning the battle against abortion while alienating people from Christ represents a Pyrrhic victory—the cost of winning the battle is so great that the war for the hearts and minds of civilization is lost.

Before developing a pro-life strategy which targets the minds and hearts of people, there must be an understanding of the different methods of applying pro-life beliefs. An old adage says, "The whole is greater than the sum of its parts." While this is generally true, each part must be in its proper place for the whole to be greater. For the pro-life movement to have a greater effect than the sum of its parts, there must be a unity of purpose, a cooperation despite differences in methods and tactics on behalf of the unborn, and a working side by side. Rising above fractionalization and infighting is necessary to develop and implement a strategy which effectively saves the lives of unborn babies. There is room for disagreement on tactics, but the goal of permanent and substantial changes in the way society approaches the abortion issue must not be forgotten.

Arguing Shared Values

Certain pro-life tactics not only are ineffective in changing people's minds about abortion, but they also turn people away from Christianity in the process. A glaring example is the tendency to use strictly religious arguments to convince nonreligious people that abortion is wrong. Reliance on religious arguments—whether sound or unsound—generally has no discernible effect on secularists, other than perhaps giving them more reason to remain nonreligious. It is sadly ironic that such a common pro-life tactic has minimal success on the temporal abortion issue but has a major role in keeping Christianity from penetrating society.

Rather than the exclusive use of religious arguments against abortion, pro-life tactics should incorporate and emphasize biological arguments against abortion. Many former "pro-choice" activists have found these compelling enough to change camps, without the need to resort to religious reasons. For example, the argument that the human spirit enters the body at conception is scientifically unprovable. But to say a separate human being is created at conception is a biological fact. The union of sperm and egg, called a *zygote*, is human because it is not animal, mineral, or vegetable, and bears a separate genetic code unique to humans. It is a being because it's alive. Apart from religion, biology affirms that life is a continuum, beginning at conception. The need to protect such life beyond conception logically follows.

Another nonreligious argument for protecting the unborn is the human rights approach. The American Declaration of Independence says, "All men are created equal and . . . endowed by their Creator with certain inalienable rights and that among these are life, liberty and the pursuit of happiness." The inalienable right to life is endowed by God, not government, yet secular courts and governments have recognized such a right. One such example is the decision of the Federal Constitutional Court of the Federal Republic of Germany—a country which all too well knows the consequences of devaluating human life. The court, two years after the United States Supreme Court decided *Roe v. Wade*, came to the conclusion that the state had a duty to protect unborn human life. The protection includes attacks on the unborn from the state as well as from individuals (including the mother). The court held that the duty to protect the unborn takes precedence even over the pregnant woman's right to self-determination:

> The right to life is guaranteed to everyone who "lives," no distinction can be made here between various stages of the life developing itself before birth, or between unborn and born life. "Everyone" in the sense of Article 2, Paragraph 2, Sentence 1, of the Basic Law is "everyone living"; expressed in another way: every life possessing human individuality, "everyone" also includes the yet unborn human being.[1]

Arguing Without Condemnation

A second glaring error of pro-life Christians is the harsh condemnation generally heaped upon women who have had abortions. This is not to suggest that women who have undergone abortions should be praised, nor should anyone feel reluctant to speak out on the wrongfulness of abortion. But women who have had abortions are often victims of exploitation (whether by boyfriends, husbands, parents, abortion clinic "counselors," or abortionists).

Criticism and condemnation tend to bring about defensiveness. Many women today are abortion-rights activists because they have been put on the defensive by opponents of abortions. In order to survive the often-severe attacks from pro-lifers, women have banded together with like-minded people. These groups provide reassurance that the decision to abort was not only okay but was the right thing to do. Unless women are willing to face their inner feelings, which often tell them that it was wrong to allow their unborn child to be killed, such women must vigorously oppose those with contrary views. Who can blame these women for denial if the alternative is enduring the hypercriticism of pro-lifers?

Instead of judgment and condemnation, pro-lifers should express understanding and compassion. The Scriptures provide people with the chance for a new beginning, with the power to avoid repeating the mistakes of the past. Should not this same opportunity, together with the forgiveness of failures, be provided to women who have had abortions? Jesus told the woman caught in adultery, "Neither do I condemn you; go your way. From now on sin no more" (John 8:11). It's time to tell women who have undergone abortions the same thing.

Arguing with Appropriate Terminology

The lack of journalistic objectivity relative to the abortion debate is staggering. The clearest example is in the terminology employed to discuss the respective sides of the issue. "Pro-life," the desired term for those who want to protect the unborn, is generally stated in the negative: "anti-abortion." This is still preferable to the contrived expression "anti-choice," which is commonly used by abortion rights zealots. However, when broadcasters or print "journalists" employ such terms as "anti-choice," the wall has been breached between reporting and rhetoric, resulting in outright advocacy.

Allowing such biased reporting to remain unchallenged effectively grants the "pro-choice" side the right to frame the issue. And as the adage says, "The one who frames the question controls the debate." It is only fair to expect and demand symmetry in the terminology used in the abortion issue. Therefore, for those who are truly interested in changing people's minds about abortion, there must be a willingness to speak out against unfair, biased, or misleading use of terminology by media and by abortion-rights activists.

If society's attitude toward abortion is going to change in the area of affording rights and protection to the unborn, the language employed in the abortion debate must be carefully chosen. Too often the terms of the debate are not only slanted to undermine the intent of the pro-life position (e.g., "anti-choice"), but are intentionally obscured to prevent people from abhorring the "pro-choice" view. For example, even the word "abortion" itself avoids dealing with the humanity of the unborn. Missions are aborted, takeoffs and landings can be aborted, but when a pregnancy is aborted, a living human being dies. Thus, "termination of a pregnancy" (i.e., "abortion") describes the procedure relative to the woman. The identity of a separate human life inside the womb is hidden within the all-encompassing term "pregnancy."

The stigma of the effect of the abortion procedure upon the fetus is avoided by the use of such abstract or undeveloped notions as "abortion" and "pregnancy." Aborting what? Pregnant with what? Since abortion kills unborn human beings, the regular substitution of "the killing of unborn human beings" for the term "abortion" would bring the right-to-life debate out of the shadows and into the light. And whatever respect and acceptance people have for the right to choose an abstract procedure will diminish with the exposure of the true nature of abortion.

Abortion rights advocates not only benefit from the employment of such abstract and undeveloped terms as "abortion" and "termination of pregnancy," but also from the expression "pro-choice." As a general rule, who isn't for "choice"? People want to be free to choose their religion, candidates for political office, spouses, friends, occupation, etc. Choice is fundamental to a free society. But "choice" has its limits. A person may have the power and ability to drive 100 miles per hour the wrong way down a one-way street. But that person doesn't have the right to act in such a manner because other persons are negatively affected through the exercise of such a "choice." Thus, no one could seriously claim to be "pro-choice" if the question were whether a person ought to have the right to choose to speed the wrong direction on a one-way street.

Since the right to choose should be determined by just what it is that is being chosen, the abstract notion of "choice" as it relates to the abortion question needs to be developed. In the abortion debate, when people say they are "pro-choice," one must ask, "Choice to decide what?" There must be an insistence that the question be answered. The answer is, of course, the choice of a pregnant woman either to kill or not kill her unborn baby.

By either helping or forcing people to explain the significance of the abstract idea of "choice," the concrete consequences of abortion are kept within the abortion debate. For example, references to "choice to kill" brings the discussion back to reality and prevents abortion rights advocates from hiding behind abstract terms. It may also be helpful to point out that of the three human beings (minimum—more if twins or triplets, etc.) involved in a pregnancy (father, mother, baby), abortion-rights advocates only extend "choice" to one: the woman. This is generally justified by the response that a woman has the right to her own body. Yes, she does, generally speaking. But a woman's right to her own body, as with the general idea of "choice," is not absolute. A woman cannot, in virtually every state of the United States, use her body for prostitution. A woman cannot ingest illegal drugs into her body. Furthermore, in the case of a pregnancy there is another human body within the pregnant woman's body. The "right to choose" abortion means the right to choose the death of an unborn human being for the convenience of the putative mother.

Long on Words, Short on Facts

The apostle Paul in his Epistle to the Romans (10:2) speaks of having "a zeal...but not in accordance with knowledge." The tragic significance of this relative to the issue of abortion is clear: Good intentions and a zeal for the unborn are not substitutes for the compelling facts which support the right-to-life position. These facts include fetal development and public sentiment regarding abortion.

The union (conception) of the male sperm and the female egg (ovum) is called a zygote. The zygote is a separate, genetically unique one-celled individual. Every bit of information needed for this tiny life to grow into a fully mature human being is already present. Six to twelve hours after conception or "fertilization," the zygote begins the process of cell growth and division. During the next three or four days the developing baby becomes implanted in the mother's womb (uterus), which serves as home for the next 260 days. From the time of implantation up until the third month of pregnancy, the unborn baby is called an *embryo*. From the third month on it is called a *fetus*.

By the time the tiny, developing human is 18-25 days old, long before the woman is sure or sometimes even aware that she is pregnant, the unborn baby's heart is already beating. At 40 days into the pregnancy, brain function can be recorded and the first movements of the unborn occur. By the time the woman is eight weeks pregnant, the heartbeat of the fetus can be heard.

An alarming fact is that most abortions take place after the unborn baby's heart is beating and brain waves can be measured. This is the type of information that abortion advocates generally either suppress, ignore, or distort (if they themselves have ever been presented with the facts of fetal development, which should not be assumed). One of the commonly employed tactics of abortion-rights proponents is the dehumanization of the unborn humans. This is accomplished through the use of terms (hardly euphemisms) such as "product of conception," "conceptus," "fetal tissue," or even "blobs of tissue." The only real difference between "blobs of tisssue" and their critics is maturity, since both are genetically human. Without interference with the maturing of these "blobs of tissue," in a few months they will be called sons and daughters, and in 18 years, voters!

It is a modern phenomenon in America to use opinion polls not only for determining how the public views an issue but also to change the way people think about issues. This is done by means of carefully worded questions which are designed to evoke a particular response. For example, if abortion-rights advocates wanted to show the popularity of the "pro-choice" view, questions could be asked such as these:

— Does every woman have the right to control her own body?

— Do you believe that a pregnant 12-year-old girl who is a victim of incest should be forced to continue her pregnancy?

— Should victims of rape resulting in pregnancy be forced to reproduce?

If a person answers yes to any of the three questions, one could conclude that the person "believes in abortion rights," is "pro-choice," and "believes in reproductive freedom."

On the other hand, sanctity-of-life advocates might ask questions similar to these:

— Do you support the use of abortion for birth control?

— Should a pregnant woman have the right to kill her unborn baby girl because the woman wanted a boy?

— Should laws protect a woman's right to kill her unborn child for any reason up through the ninth month of pregnancy?

Answering no to any of the latter set could be deemed "pro-life," "anti-abortion," or "pro abortion-restrictions." Before believing the "results" of polls on the abortion issue, it is crucial to understand who conducted the poll, who (if anyone) commissioned the poll, what questions were asked, and how they were asked.

The *Los Angeles Times*, hardly a "conservative" or "pro-life" newspaper, conducted a nationwide telephone poll in early March 1989. In what is one of the largest and most substantive surveys ever conducted on the issue of abortion, more than 3500 American adults were interviewed. This number included a national cross-section sample of more than 2400 people, plus an additional "oversample" of more than 1100 women. The oversample of women was to provide greater statistical precision to their opinions expressed, but their answers were "weighted" so that the overall survey would represent a normal percentage mix of men and women. The results:

> 61% believe abortion is "morally wrong"
> (22% believe it is "morally right")
>
> 57% think "abortion is murder" (a third of the women polled who have had abortions considered it "murder")
> (35% do not think it is murder)
>
> 80% oppose abortion as a form of birth control
> (13% favor abortion for birth control)
>
> 57% oppose the idea that "a woman should be able to get an abortion no matter what the reason"
> (34% believe a woman should be able to obtain an abortion for any reason)

Despite the fact that Americans generally consider abortion immoral, a majority of those interviewed did approve of abortion in certain exceptional situations:

> 88% approve of abortion "when a woman's health is seriously endangered"
> (6% oppose abortion in such cases)
>
> 84% approve of abortion "if a woman became pregnant as a result of rape or incest"
> (10% oppose abortion in such cases)
>
> 74% approve of abortion "if there is a strong chance of serious defect in the baby"
> (17% oppose abortion in such cases)

As the reasons for abortion become less compelling, the majority oppose it:

> 49% oppose abortion "if the family has a very low income and cannot afford any more children" (41% favor abortion in such cases)

> 51% oppose abortion "if an unmarried woman who is pregnant does not want to marry that man" (40% favor abortion in such cases)

> 54% oppose abortion "if she is married and does not want any more children" (36% favor abortion in such cases)

Those who favor abortion tend to have generally liberal views on "family values," think motherhood can often be a burden, want to change women's status in society, and don't feel that a woman's place is in the home. They also support homosexual rights. Abortion-rights advocates tend to have fewer children, and the majority are either separated, remarried, or divorced. They consider religion less important in their lives and tend to be Jewish or to attend religious services only occasionally.

Those surveyed who oppose abortion believe the country is in a state of moral decline and hold traditional, conservative views on "family values." They feel a woman's place is in the home and motherhood is a woman's most important and satisfying role. Abortion opponents have more children than average, consider religion very important in their lives, and regularly or frequently attend religious services.

Of the women surveyed who have had abortions, 56 percent said they felt "a sense of guilt about having had an abortion," and 26 percent said they now "mostly regret the abortion."

The *Boston Globe*/WBZ TV poll, conducted March 27-29, 1989, reveals the same basic results as the *Los Angeles Times* poll. The *Globe*, a strongly "pro-choice" newspaper, wrote: "While 78% of the nation would keep abortion legal in limited circumstances, these circumstances count for a tiny percentage of the reasons cited by women having abortions."

The *Globe* went on to say, "When pregnancy results from rape or incest, when the mother's physical health is endangered, and when there is likely to be a genetic deformity of the fetus, those queried strongly approve of legal abortions. But when pregnancy poses financial or emotional strain, or when the woman is alone or a teenager, the reasons that are given by most women seeking abortions, an overwhelming majority of Americans believe that abortion should be illegal."

Contrary to misleading perceptions of public feelings about abortion, as the *Boston Globe* stated, "Most Americans would ban the vast majority of abortions performed in this country." Even when a "loaded" question is asked which suggests a "pro-choice answer"—such as the *Los Angeles Times* poll question "Does every woman have the right to control her own body?"—only 51 percent agreed. Americans, therefore, overwhelmingly oppose 98 percent of the abortions performed. The remaining 2 percent of abortions—those due to maternal health, rape, incest, or fetal defects (the hard cases)—are favored by a majority of Americans. This means that most Americans are "pro-life" and generally opposed to abortion, with exceptions permitted for the "hard cases."

Activism Through Alternatives

If the Christian message and its application to life is going to penetrate society, proper actions of believers must accompany the message. It is easy to accuse religions of hypocrisy, and it is unfortunate that enough inconsistencies and contradictions exist in the lives of professing believers to make the charges appear valid. When it comes to the abortion issue, the societal perception of Christianity is not enhanced when "pro-life" Christians talk about alternatives to abortion but fail to take steps to provide meaningful alternatives. This benign neglect affords the secularist an opportunity to recite the oft-heard, "They don't practice what they preach." Not only does the non-Christian question the sincerity of the "pro-life" position in such cases, but the issue could be raised as to whether the Christian faith itself is a convenient philosophy of "all talk and no action." Active participation in the practice of Christianity is the only way to reach a secular world with the truth and the fruit of the gospel.

Women who are involved in unplanned, "crisis" pregnancies are physically and emotionally affected. In such a heightened state of turmoil, women need understanding and assistance, rather than condemnation. A common criticism of the pro-life movement, whether true or false, is that little care is shown for the woman, and concern for the child ends once the baby is born. If the pro-life movement is to make progress in the quest to end abortion, both the needs of the woman (pre and postpartum) and those of the born child must be addressed.

The physical needs of a pregnant woman include medical assistance, food, and housing. If the inability to afford the cost of prenatal care and delivery is the main reason that many women choose abortion, low- or no-cost medical services have to be made available. This may seem like a formidable task, but the number of visible pro-life obstetricians and gynecologists is increasing, and many are willing to donate time to help the indigent, poor, or otherwise at-risk women. A model of what can be done is the Living Well Medical Clinic in Orange, California, where on-site pregnancy tests are offered, as well as low-cost or no-cost prenatal services. This physician-staffed center is a privately funded pro-life clinic. It has successfully counseled and provided services for hundreds of pregnant women who were considering abortion but chose life for their babies instead. Many similar pro-life centers exist across America, but more are needed. Every city ought to have such a place, which would not only provide affordable medical care, but would also eliminate a common reason for choosing abortion.

Many pregnant women feel that in order to avoid homelessness an abortion is necessary. Whether the result of threats from parents, boyfriends, or husbands, women often are told to "abort or else live on the street." Such an ultimatum which threatens the well-being of the pregnant woman is not easily resisted. The pressure of worrying about homelessness or abandonment by family and lovers is enough for many women to choose abortion despite a desire to bring their babies to term. In such difficult circumstances, temporary housing provided by caring pro-life individuals has been the difference between life and death for the unborn baby.

Unless sufficient housing is available which meets the needs of the pregnant woman during the time of family or housing crisis, then "pro-life" preachment is merely rhetoric, lacking in practical and meaningful ways to give women the means to choose life. If every church had at least one or two parishioners who designated a "pro-life bedroom" within their homes, women in crisis pregnancies would have a solution to their housing crisis. The church as a whole could donate clothing (including baby clothes), food, and emotional support to the mothers-to-be. Instead of condemnation and rejection, women would find the acceptance and love which protects human dignity and provides an incentive to endure whatever difficulties may exist.

Both the woman and the baby have needs which arise after the birth has taken place. For the woman, help with household maintenance (and often with other siblings) is a godsend. The hormonal and physical changes which occur after delivery can be more easily endured by having friends serve as "sounding boards" and "safety valves" when pressures build. It is difficult enough to try to meet the constant demands of a baby when the mother is tired, run-down, and stressed-out. But when the mother feels she is "going it alone" with no relief in sight, a hopeless despair can easily trigger deep depression, placing both mother and baby at risk for serious psychological and physical consequences.

Women may not be able to avoid all the possible difficulties connected with raising babies, but women should not have to face the challenges alone. If committed pro-life people were available for both mother and newborn baby, lending practical assistance where necessary, even pregnant women in the most difficult circumstances would be inclined to choose life over abortion.

For pro-lifers to avoid criticisms which hinder both pro-life and gospel efforts, providing the basic necessities (i.e., food, shelter, medical attention) for pregnant women is a must. But beyond the immediate needs, long-term planning and assistance is vital. For example, providing education and training for pregnant women enables them to avoid permanent or even temporary reliance on the government. Biblical teaching about sexuality and morality (in the case of unwed mothers) gives women the moral reasons to avoid the type of activity which results in an unplanned pregnancy. And education about responsible family planning and the proper use of birth control methods can prevent future crisis pregnancies. Finally, employment opportunities, together with child-care assistance, help women to attain and continue self-sufficiency. Few people would reject opportunities to regain control over their own lives. Basic necessities must be available to sustain women through pregnancy crises, but long-range planning and training must exist for pro-life alternatives to be more than a "quick fix." Since mothers and babies are important, "sanctity of life" concerns must lead to "quality of life" attention for both mother and baby after the birth takes place. This holistic approach is the only way to legitimately claim that the pro-life movement provides "alternatives" to abortion.

Activism Through Actions

An unsettling but perhaps understandable result from the *Los Angeles Times* poll involved unmarried women's feelings about adoption. Asked whether it would be harder for an unmarried woman to rear a child out of wedlock, give up the baby for adoption, or have an abortion, 52 percent said the "hardest" thing would be to give up the infant for adoption. Only 18 percent said the hardest thing under such circumstances would be abortion. When women consider it easier to abort than allow adoption, something is terribly wrong. Herein lies one of the greatest opportunities for pro-lifers to convince pregnant women to choose life. The attitude that says, "If I can't raise the child myself, I'll choose to kill it," is not only illogical, but could also be applied to born children which are a burden to a family in crisis.

Since millions of Americans have been successfully adopted, why is there so little mention of the alternative of loving, adoptive parents ready, willing, and able to commit their lives to raising a child as their own? The abortion-rights rhetoric focuses on "children of color" (i.e., minorities) and handicapped babies as being "unwanted." Whether or not that's true (although "unwanted" is extreme—"more difficult to place" is more accurate), such infants are but a small (albeit important) percentage of the children placed for adoption. Rather than dwelling on the difficulty in placing some babies for adoption, the opportunity to give life instead of death to an unborn baby, together with the overwhelmingly good prospects of adopted children, should be the emphasis. And pro-life families should seriously consider whether they could accommodate a child in need of a family.

Many communities have pro-life organizations which provide free pregnancy testing, counseling, and referrals to pregnant women for housing, medical attention, and economic assistance. These organizations are generally called "crisis pregnancy centers" and are staffed and supported by pro-life people who choose to get involved. A good starting point in pro-life involvement is to find out whether a Crisis Pregnancy Center (CPC) exists in your community. If one (or more) does exist, find out the name, location, and phone number (many CPCs are listed in phone directories—ask your pastor, priest, or pro-life activist if you need help). Next, call the CPC (or better yet, stop by) and find out all you can about the services it provides. Then decide what you are able to do to help (phone counseling, fund-raising, bookkeeping, etc.) Finally, give of your time, energy, and resources.

Whether done with or through a pro-life organization, sidewalk counseling is the last line of defense before a woman fulfills her "choice" of abortion. Most pregnant women are ill at ease when arriving at an abortion clinic. Hence, they are extremely vulnerable to abuse, whether it comes from the biological father, the clinic staff, or "pro-lifers" at the scene. It is one thing to be adamantly pro-life. It is quite another to hurl insults or words of condemnation at women who themselves are usually victims of circumstances.

Sidewalk counselors have the opportunity to inform women of the alternatives to abortion at a time when many women want to know that "choice" means more than the abortion option. Furthermore, many women claim that they were ignorant of the facts of fetal development and the psychological effects which often show up in women after they've had an abortion. Thus the sidewalk counselor has a chance to provide women with information which could help them avoid actions they might later regret. Sidewalk counseling should therefore be done by knowledgeable, committed, and caring women and men who are as concerned with the woman as with the unborn baby. Hundreds of babies are saved every year through the efforts of those who provide living alternatives at the door of death.

Operation Rescue

Civil disobedience is biblically required where government authorities order Christians to do what the Bible forbids or forbid Christians from doing what Scripture commands (Acts 5:29—"We must obey God rather than men"). A clear example is in Acts chapter 5 where the Sanhedrin (Jewish Supreme Court) ordered the apostles to stop proclaiming the death and resurrection of Jesus. The apostles responded by saying it was a mandate to obey God, therefore man-made edicts must be subordinated to divine commands (Acts 5:29). What is not so clear is how, if at all, this applies to the abortion question.

Not only can the Bible be understood as requiring the breaking of trespassing and other laws in order to save the lives of unborn babies ("Deliver those who are being taken away to death"—Proverbs 24:11), many juries have agreed that trespassing is justified when it is done in an attempt to save a life. However, this is an extremely gray area of both law and biblical interpretation. No definitive answer exists. Tactics should therefore reflect one's personal convictions as to the Scripture and law. Efforts must be designed to maximize the chances of changing the minds of pregnant women without hardening them against a pro-life point of view and alienating them from Christianity. Each pro-life person must decide which pro-life activities and tactics are appropriate and justified. And those who choose to condemn certain pro-lifers for their tactics had better have their own "string of fish to show." It is one thing for actively involved pro-lifers to critique certain pro-life tactics. It is quite another for criticism to come from professed "pro-lifers" who themselves are doing nothing on behalf of the unborn or pregnant women.

Activism: Your Choice

By now the need is evident for something far beyond mental assent to Christianity and the pro-life movement. It is only natural for those who have remained on the sidelines to feel uncomfortable with maintaining such a "safe perspective," keeping a safe distance from the fray. But the time has arrived for action. Are you comfortable with laws which permit abortion up until the moment of birth? Do you mind subsidizing abortion with money you paid in taxes? Do you feel revulsion when hearing of the abortionist on my radio show tell of the case of one of his patients who had just received her thirty-ninth abortion (the woman was 28 years old!)? Finally, are you troubled by abortion as a means of birth control or gender selection, especially when the majority of all abortions are performed after an unborn baby's heart is beating and brain waves can be measured? If none of these things bother you, that is your choice. But don't complain when you receive judgment for an apathetic, unfeeling, and uncaring abdication to the dehumanizing practice of abortion on demand. The familiar words of Pastor Martin Niemoller regarding why Protestants didn't oppose the Nazis are timely:

> In Germany they came first for the Communists. I didn't speak up because I wasn't a Communist. Then they came for the Jews, and I didn't speak up, because I wasn't a Jew. Then they came for the Catholics, and I didn't speak up, because I was a Protestant. Then they came for me, and by that time there was no one left to speak up for anyone.[2]

The battle and the war against abortion are winnable. But consistent, active involvement by knowledgeable, committed, and caring people is the only way to protect the unborn while making an impact upon society with a gospel of Christ's love and forgiveness.

11

AIDS, Homosexuals, Junkies: Compassion with an Asterisk

Consider the following scenario: An injured man, obviously hurting and scared, limps through glass double doors into a hospital emergency room. A nurse, seeing the man, tells him to sit down. The nurse asks the man two questions:

1. What is the nature of your medical problem?
2. How did your problem arise?

The injured man asks for clarification regarding the second question. "Are you asking what conduct on my part may have brought about my problem?" the man queries. The nurse replies, "Yes, did you do anything to cause your problem?"

At this point the patient, despite considerable pain, becomes indignant. He wants to know why it is necessary for the emergency room staff to know how he became injured. The nurse proceeds to point to a large sign on the wall, which states in large print:

We have committed our lives to healing people.
We seek to provide the finest medical assistance possible.

We do not discriminate on the basis of race, color, creed, religion, gender, or national origin.*

As the injured man finishes reading the sign, he sees it. There it is, right at the end of the large print. Immediately following the words "or national origin." It is an asterisk. Unmistakable. Plain as day. The patient looks beneath the large print with the asterisk and sees a second asterisk followed by fine print. Squinting, he makes out the text of the tiny letters:

> *Except when a patient's medical condition arises from the patient's own conduct which the emergency room staff deems immoral or inappropriate. We hereby reserve the right to refuse service to anyone.

At this point the patient protests, stating forcefully that it shouldn't matter how someone's condition arose. He rises to leave, but before limping out the double doors exclaims, "I'm going somewhere else for treatment. I suggest that you decide whether you're in the healing business or not."

In making the transition from a hospital emergency room to the church, the Bible calls the church to provide spiritual and emotional healing—healing of minds, souls, emotions . . . the calling to be ministers, counselors, encouragers. The church is the divine emergency room, staffed by those willing to offer help to all who are suffering—not selectively, and certainly not conditioned upon people having an "acceptable" problem or having acquired their problem in an acceptable way. If the church is going to increase its impact on society, there must be a manifestation of unconditional compassion for the afflicted. The Bible mandates such compassion. The church must get rid of the asterisks. Either the church is in the healing business or it isn't.

Compassion Without Discrimination

The prophet Zechariah exhorted the Jews to "practice kindness and compassion each to his brother" (Zechariah 7:9). Those who desire to follow the living God have no option. The following verse provides the scope of such compassion: "Do not oppress the widow or the orphan, the stranger or the poor" (Zechariah 7:10). As Zechariah laments the failure of God's people to fulfill this challenge to be compassionate, it is noteworthy that he specifically mentions the "stranger." It is certainly human nature to gravitate toward those of like mind and like belief. But the test of one's compassion is how well one treats those who look, believe, and act differently, especially when a repugnant life-style or practice is the direct cause of their need for compassion. Whether it's a drug addict in a self-induced stupor or a homosexual suffering the ravages of the AIDS virus, practicing unconditional compassion is a requirement for true believers.

Instead of compassion for those involved in immoral life-styles, the church too often expresses contempt. Is it any wonder that those caught up in immorality tend to band together for support, establishing their own communities and circle of friends who share the commonality of unbiblical behavior? Beyond this, the church is perceived as the enemy—responsible for perpetuating the stigma which attaches to certain behavior without offering any hope. Since the Bible nowhere speaks of the "ministry of condemnation," perhaps it is time to recheck attitudes and actions which attack hurting people rather than reaching out to them in love.

When Jesus went through the cities and villages, He offered hope for both the temporal and eternal problems of the people. This was done by healing the people from every kind of disease and every kind of sickness, plus presenting the gospel of the kingdom (Matthew 9:35). Did Christ see this as an interference with His more important mission of becoming God's sacrifice for sin? Did He selectively choose whom to heal, condemning those whose practices contributed to their problems? In direct contrast to the unfortunate attitudes frequently expressed by the contemporary church, "seeing the multitudes, He felt compassion for them, because they were distressed and downcast like sheep without a shepherd" (Matthew 9:36). No discrimination, no exceptions, no asterisks.

For the church to regain its position of influence in the lives of individuals and in society as a whole, she must abide by biblical admonitions. Although it is easier to begin and end with expressions of revulsion and condemnation, which tend to be natural, automatic reactions toward certain immoral life-styles and practices, the church has not been called out to be natural or to engage in automatic reactions. Instead, Christians are called to live on a plane above the "natural, since the natural man does not accept the things of the Spirit of God, for they are foolishness to him, and he cannot understand them, because they are spiritually appraised" (1 Corinthians 2:14). Responding to those who are following their baser desires with attitudes of contempt, disgust, and criticism only makes the problem greater, widening the gap between the "healers" of Christianity and the ones the church is called to heal.

Hanging in the Balance:
Compassion and Conviction

If indeed the church is called to be a healer without regard to the manner in which people's hurts arise, does this mean an abandonment of convictions about proper behavior? It is difficult to ignore, for example, the fact that some 80 percent of people in the United States infected with HIV (human immunodeficiency virus—the virus that causes AIDS) acquired the virus through homosexual contact, sex with a prostitute, or intravenous drug abuse. Since these behaviors are not biblically acceptable, how do the convictions that certain practices are immoral affect the need to express unconditional compassion?

Conviction without compassion is a cold, sterile, condemnatory type of legalism. This approach is indicative of the Pharisees of Jesus' day who acted like self-appointed moral watchdogs without concern for the needs of the people. Such an attitude reflects a desire to defend the character of God at any cost, disregarding people who are created in God's image. Perhaps there would be less need to defend God's character if the church exemplified the divine character, including the attribute of compassion.

But compassion without conviction is itself a subtle snare. This approach ignores underlying spiritual problems, of which a disease such as AIDS may be a symptom. As a result, there is an unwillingness or inability to deal with a person's relationship with God and failure to present God's blueprint for right living. Hence, the most important work of the church—that of preparing people for eternity through acceptance of Christ's finished work on the cross— is avoided through benign neglect.

Without convictions which confront the spiritual roots of problems, compassion for human suffering is, at best, palliative. Like giving painkillers to people with cancer, masking the symptoms often leads to the denial of any deeper, more serious problems. At worst, compassion without conviction is deceptive, offering temporal soothing as a false hope to a terminal condition.

If the church is here merely to be a genteel, convictionless accommodator of rebellious and sinful behavior, perhaps it's time to recheck the mission of the church. Soothing, pious flummery may indeed help get people through the day. But if that is the primary focus of the church's practices—getting people through the day—why bother with Christianity? Why not choose a remedy which avoids the doctrinaire, divisive moral pronouncements and tenets of faith inherent in the Christian religion?

Drugs can get people through the day. So can a positive mental attitude, self-indulgence, self-hypnosis, and even negative emotions such as hatred and revenge. There are innumerable distractions and niceties which can get people's minds off their pain, suffering, and misery and help get them through the day. The mission of the church, however, is to get people through eternity while maintaining a compassionate concern for the problems of the day. It's not either "compassion or conviction." It's both "compassion *and* conviction," biblically balanced to minister to temporal and eternal needs.

The church should no more avoid dealing with the spiritual roots of unbiblical behavior than a medical doctor would avoid dealing with the roots of an organic disease. A compassionate desire to soothe temporal pain finds its maximum effect only when tempered by asserting convictions which address the root of the problem.

Correcting the Imbalance of Conviction and Compassion

The story of the woman caught in adultery serves to present the right and wrong ways to balance conviction and compassion:

> And everyone went to his home. But Jesus went to the Mount of Olives. And early in the morning He came again into the temple, and all the people were coming to Him; and He sat down and began to teach them. And the scribes and the Pharisees brought a woman caught in adultery, and having set her in the midst, they said to Him, "Teacher, this woman has been caught in adultery, in the very act. Now in the law Moses commanded us to stone such women; what then do You say?" And they were saying this, testing Him, in order that they might have grounds for accusing Him. But Jesus stooped down, and with His finger wrote on the ground. But when they persisted in asking Him, He straightened up, and said to them, "He who is without sin among you, let him be the first to throw a stone at her."

And again He stooped down, and wrote on the ground. And when they heard it, they began to go out one by one, beginning with the older ones, and He was left alone, and the woman, where she had been, in the midst. And straightening up, Jesus said to her, "Woman, where are they? Did no one condemn you?" And she said, "No one, Lord." And Jesus said, "Neither do I condemn you; go your way; from now on sin no more" (John 7:53–8:11).

The Pharisees were separationists who had shunned the common people of Israel. The Pharisees saw themselves as a "cut above," favored by God for their hairsplitting obedience to His law. They also had a warped view of sin (they hardly considered their own arrogance and pride to be wrong). These factors, plus a burning contempt for the purity, impact, and following of Jesus, set the stage for one of many attempts by the Pharisees to trap Him.

The wrong way to combine conviction and compassion is clearly seen in the Pharisees' reaction to the woman caught in adultery. First, they were insincere. Rather than a genuine concern for protecting the divinely ordained sanctity of marriage, the true reason for the Pharisees bringing the adulteress to Jesus was to turn the people against Him. Under the guise of wanting a biblical resolution to the situation with the woman, the Pharisees thought they had Jesus trapped. They presented the Mosaic commandment that such a person should be stoned, then asked, "What then do You say?" (John 8:5).

Furthermore, the Pharisees were lacking in compassion. The woman was not only a pawn in their attempt to snare Jesus, but she also was set up for judgment and condemnation without regard to compassion. Playing the role of watchdogs, the Pharisees were ready to attack and destroy the violators of God's law, disregarding such factors as love, healing, and restoration. The focus wasn't on the needs of the people. Instead, the Pharisees vigorously pursued a moral symmetry, treating people as disposable commodities once they stepped out of line. It is frightening to think how pervasive this Pharisaic attitude is in the modern church era.

Finally, the Pharisees were hypocritical. They ignored their own failures but were selectively fixated on the sins of others. Being a sinner doesn't disqualify someone from confronting sin in others. In fact, if Christians waited until they were sinlessly perfect to take a stand against sin, there would be no one standing. But the Pharisees' zeal in searching out marital infidelity was a mere pretext for attacking anyone and anything which believed or practiced differently than they. Their own sin was conveniently ignored so that they could continue to stoke their fires of pseudo-righteous indignation. Lack of compassion combined with misguided conviction represents the true nature of the approach of the Pharisees.

In the ostensible dilemma of choosing between condemnation ("stone her") and antinomianism ("let her go"), the church has been largely seduced. Instead of recognizing a third alternative (called in logic "escaping through the horns of the dilemma"), the church opts for one or the other extreme. For example, many Christians feel justified in telling AIDS victims, "You made your bed, now go and sleep in it. You reap what you sow" (the equivalent of "Stone the adulterous woman"). Others might tell the practicing homosexual, drug addict, or habitual procurer of prostitutes, "You're okay as you are—everything is fine" (the equivalent of "Let the woman go").

Jesus neither says "Kill her" nor "Let her go." Instead, He tells the Pharisees and scribes to "go ahead and stone her—but only if you're in a moral position to do so" (i.e., "without sin"). Jesus freely offered to the one who had never misused God-given sexual desires the opportunity to launch the first salvo. In one sentence, Jesus puts their indignation into a context which exposes their hypocrisy and avoidance of self-examination.

But Jesus didn't stop with His writing in the dust and the exodus of the scribes and Pharisees. He turned to the woman, now without accusers, and pronounced her free of condemnation. However, He tempered His compassion and forgiveness with conviction, adding the strongest of warnings: "Go and sin no more." In clear terms He told her to stop the practice that brought her into the present situation. There was no condemnation of her as a person, but the practice (adultery) *is* condemned. And it is strongly implied that continuation of the condemned practice will lead to judgment upon her as a person.

The Application of Conviction for Believers

In order both to avoid the errors of the scribes and Pharisees and imitate the example of Jesus, certain practices must be maintained—for example, the call to exercise unconditional love. If a person professing to be a Christian cannot sincerely love people due to their past or present behavior, it is questionable whether that person ought to be considered a true Christian. The requirements of authentic Christianity are not easy to accomplish. God loved us while we were His enemies, in open rebellion against Him (Romans 5:8-10). Jesus amplified the commandment to love by exhorting His followers to love "as I have loved you" (John 13:34). Unconditional love is the standard, and believers are able to develop this type of love because God sincerely loved us first (1 John 4:19). The knowledge and acceptance of God's love becomes the means to sincerely love others. This is especially true when certain people who are more difficult to love become the beneficiaries of Christian love. What greater example of love exists on the human level than the sincere offer of eternal life to those without hope in this life? Properly applied convictions never lose sight of sincere love and concern.

Life is but a vapor, here one day and gone the next; and, generally speaking, no one knows when the end will come. But some people because of sickness and disease are known to have fewer days remaining than most. It is these people who are most in greater need of the dignity God has bestowed upon humanity. It is the suffering and the terminally ill who have a superior need to hear the conviction that there's an eternal weight of glory which far outweighs present suffering (2 Corinthians 4:16-18). A perspective which emphasizes the eternal instead of the temporal affords the dying person the opportunity to face eternity with hope and dignity. This is compassion balanced with conviction.

The fact that all have sinned (Romans 3:23), thereby earning judgment from God (Roman 6:23), is tempered by the fact that forgiveness is available. The judicial fact of sin demands punishment for the offense. But the death of Christ for all offenders, whereby He bore the penalty and punishment for the sins of many, becomes the means for acceptance of the sinner by God. Within this context no one, no matter how tried and true, has earned bragging rights. The biblical context of sin humbles the believer, eliminating any basis for a self-righteous attitude or condescension toward others. Instead, the conviction that breaking God's law is wrong and demands punishment is followed by the recognition of forgiveness to all who ask. There is much more beyond the successes and failures of this life, so the Christian conviction regarding the life hereafter must not be neglected or subdued.

When Jesus taught in the famous Sermon on the Mount to "not judge, lest you be judged" (Matthew 7:1), He was referring to harsh, critical, and hypocritical condemnation. However, He also commanded His followers, "Do not judge according to appearance, but judge with righteous judgment" (John 7:24). The command to avoid condemnation is tempered by the command to discern righteously. The compassion of Jesus is balanced by the conviction that certain practices are right and certain practices are wrong. If the church is able to balance successfully the need for compassion on the afflicted with the conviction that one's relationship with God in light of eternity is the utmost priority, then the church will fulfill its mission. Both compassion and conviction are mandates for the church. Therefore, in order to make her prescribed impact, the church must adjust its attitudes and practices to conform to the commands and example of the Lord Himself.

12

The Crisis in Christian Leadership

It is difficult to judge how successful the followers of Christ have been historically in faithfully representing Christ to the world. It is not so difficult, however, to conclude that today Christians are failing to have a significant impact on secular society. Even the most optimistic believer ought to be willing to admit that there's plenty of room for individuals and the church collectively to improve their effectiveness.

Christians are supposed to be witnesses for Christ. Increasingly, criticism is raised that we no longer reflect the Jesus of Scripture in a meaningful way. If indeed there is a "great gulf fixed" between Christ and His people, how do Christians adjust their practices to conform to the biblical calling of being Christ's witnesses (Acts 1:8)? Although there is presently no lack of good teaching and preaching which enables believers to function more productively within the present church system, it is the system itself which needs to be overhauled. A prime example is the way in which Christian "ministries" represent Christ and Christianity.

Rather than implementing the biblical exhortations to Christian practice, such as those found in the Christian classic *The Imitation of Christ* by Thomas à Kempis, "ministries" today seem to be practicing an "imitation of the world." Everything from Madison Avenue fund-raising techniques and gimmicks to bizarre and sensationalistic claims are utilized to perpetuate and expand these "ministries." Add to this the frequent arm-twisting, manipulative appeals for money, and the net effect is a circus-like environment, complete with carnival barkers. What happened to the concept that ministries are to be organizations representing a holy God?

Perceptive and courageous believers have been lamenting the existence of glitzy, Hollywood-style "ministries" for years. It was not until the 1987 "holy war" involving Jim Bakker and PTL, followed by the 1988 Jimmy Swaggart upheaval, that most Christians became aware of the potential for independent "ministries" to undermine the reputation of all of Christianity. Unfortunately, failures within the Bakker and Swaggart ministries have commonly been imputed to the church at large. Tragically, many non-Christians—and perhaps believers, too—went even further, somehow blaming Christ for the misdeeds of certain of His professed followers.

Rethinking the Call to Service

Most biblical scholars would agree that there are no discussions in the Scripture concerning para-church ministries (i.e., ministries designed to supplement the church's efforts in evangelism, discipleship, and helping the needy). This is not to say, however, that such ministries are without biblical foundation. Instead, the New Testament model has supplemental efforts of evangelism, etc., performed through the auspices of local churches. For example, the Holy Spirit set apart Paul and Barnabas for the work of evangelism, and sent them out on the first missionary journey (Acts 13:1-4). But their calling was ratified by the leaders of the church at

Antioch, who were also said to have sent out Paul and Barnabas (Acts 13:3). Thus, the calling of God to ministry was recognized and confirmed by a local church to which the ministers remained accountable.

Until the twentieth century, few Christian organizations existed apart from local churches. But with the rise of nondenominational and independent congregations in the twentieth-century, para-church ministries began to emerge. These took the form of general evangelistic organizations, campus ministries, radio and television ministries, rescue missions, relief organizations, etc. Some of these entities came about through efforts designed to utilize advances in technology for the spreading of the gospel. Others were established to meet special needs of people, both physical and spiritual. Unfortunately, still others became or even began as vehicles for charismatic personalities to fulfill personal ambitions of popularity and wealth.

The common denominators between para-church groups are essentially twofold: First, the stated purpose of the groups is to assist and supplement the work of the church; second, these ministries are not connected to any one local church or denomination.

Generally, organizations are controlled by boards which establish and maintain the direction of the ministry. Often, though, such boards are handpicked by the ministry founder, which raises questions of "rubber-stamping" the desires of the founder. Even more controversial are the boards made up by a majority of relatives of the founder. In an age of extreme skepticism toward Christianity it is only fair to question the wisdom of having such a governing structure. The burden ought to be upon ministries to prove their integrity and accountability. And Christians ought not be afraid to demand proof of organizational integrity before offering their support.

While in college, I had a discussion with a local pastor regarding the nature of the "ministry." During the discussion he mentioned a particular, well-known campus ministry, calling it a "parasite on the church." His point was that this para-church organization was feeding off the church, but giving nothing in return. Although his attitude is not typical of the way most Christians view para-church ministries, his comments reveal a deep-felt hurt and resentment, and reflect the need to reexamine the place of these ministries. Since the local church is the biblically ordained authority for the overseeing of Christian ministry, have para-church ministries usurped the role of the church?

It is perhaps fair to say that had local churches (including associations of local churches, or "denominations") done their part in properly fulfilling their ministries function, there may never have been the need for other ministries. However, regardless of the factors that gave rise to the para-church movement, there are reasons to believe that these ministries have overstepped their bounds in "supplementing" the church.

Jesus said, "I will build My church" (Matthew 16:18). The "church" is the universal body of believers who have been born again through faith in Jesus Christ. The universal church functions through local congregations called assemblies, fellowships, or local churches. Local churches, then, are the visible vehicle of ministry in the community and the hub of Christian activity. Those in need have access to the immediate, personal, and continuing assistance of believers in the community through the local church. But if competing functions of ministry are offered by para-church organizations, the natural consequence is a dilution in participation and support of the local church. Furthermore, for many believers para-church organization has become a substitute for the local church.

Rethinking Local Church Priorities

When Jesus said He would build His church (Matthew 16:18), He was endorsing the church as the organization and organism through which He would reach the world. Just as the church represents the hands of Jesus in the world, so parachurch ministries try to be the hands of the church.

Often, the church and para-church organizations have the same ministry goals. The flexibility of para-church ministries, however, together with their ability to focus on very narrow and specialized aspects of Christian service, frequently allows them to become highly efficient in their particular branch of ministry. Examples of this include Bible translation organizations, marriage and family enrichment ministries, crisis pregnancy groups, etc. Their success, however, raises a problem: With so many worthwhile and effective organizations to support, how should a Christian decide upon financially assisting worthy ministries?

When it comes to deciding who should be the recipients of contributions for ministry, the local church should come first. In fact, giving to the needy or supporting ministries beyond the church can still be done *through* the local church. The apostle Paul collected money in the city of Corinth and the region of Galatia for the destitute saints in Jerusalem. Paul's fund-raising, however, was done through the church in Corinth and the churches of Galatia (1 Corinthians 16:1-3).

Local churches are well-suited to determine for themselves which para-church ministries should be supported with resources from believers in the congregations. Whether missionary activity, relief for the poor, etc., when local churches make the decisions as to which causes to support, there is less chance of money and other resources being given to the wrong ministries for the wrong reasons.

The wisdom of believers giving their firstfruits to their local church should be apparent. And once the responsibility of supporting the church is accomplished, Christians are free to give to para-church ministries or directly to the needy and ought to do so.

Many para-church organizations are active in training believers to be better ministers, spouses, workers, etc. If the net effect of such organizations is that God is glorified and the local church is strengthened, then a legitimate function is served. Often, though, money, time, and involvement which ought to be donated to the local church is instead given over to ministries outside of the believer's community. The result can be an anemic local church, bled of its vitality by organizations which often provide little more than self-gratification and entertainment for believers, rather then opportunities to serve within the community.

The keys to supporting para-church ministries, then, include: recognizing the priority of the local church, giving with the right attitude, and being diligent in determining the worthiness and integrity of the organization designated for receiving support. If these guidelines are carefully followed, chaos, competition, and bitterness between churches and para-church ministries can be avoided.

Rethinking the Measure of Integrity

> For it is time for judgment to begin with the household of God (1 Peter 4:17).

In order to prevent excesses and scandals which fuel the unbelievers' skepticism of Christianity, safeguards must be implemented by both Christian organizations and individuals. The potential for significant failure among Christian leaders will always be present, owing to the fact that all Christians—leaders and nonleaders alike—are sinners saved by grace. However, there are ways to minimize the likelihood of great upheavals occurring. If believers are willing to demand that Christian leaders believe and act in a manner consistent with biblical teachings, the possibility of serious problems arising is greatly diminished. If biblical checks and balances are built into the structure of churches and ministries, the battle for integrity is nearly won. The threshold question, however, is whether the church—all its individuals included—is willing to take the time to understand how to test the integrity of a ministry.

Non-Christians who choose to reject the gospel due to the moral failure or inconsistency of its advocates are treading on thin ice. It makes little sense to reject a message because of the problems of the messenger unless the one who hears the message is looking for a reason to disbelieve. For such a person, the moral failure of a messenger provides a convenient excuse to reject the message. For those who care to objectively analyze the scandals of the past, the well-reported episodes involve certain prominent individuals who acted inconsistently with the faith they espoused. But the stories also include the sincere attempts by fellow believers to confront the hypocrisy once it became known.

Once most Christians became aware of the televangelist's problems, their indignation superseded that of unbelievers, showing that the church is not indifferent toward sin. However, in contrast to non-Christians and secular media, the church was also concerned with repentance, forgiveness, restitution, and restoration. It was the church and her leaders who took action to correct the problems, even though the individuals involved resisted the efforts of the church. And while the most visible and prominent were involved in failure, the majority of ministries—both church and parachurch—continued to serve the Lord with pure hearts.

Rethinking the Biblical Tests of a Ministry

1. *Is the ministry financially accountable?*

Much of the New Testament deals with the proper attitude toward material goods, especially money. Jesus said no one can serve both God and money (Matthew 6:24), and it was the practice within the early church that only established leaders were to handle money (Acts 11:29,30). Otherwise, if immoral and dishonest people were permitted access to ministry resources, the potential for disaster was tremendous. Jesus illustrated how corruption in a person's heart comes to the surface when money is involved by allowing Judas Iscariot to handle the disciples' moneybag. Judas, who had an unhealthy obsession with money, acted true to his character by pilfering from the disciples' funds (John 12:6).

As a response to the need for accountability of parachurch groups, organizations have been created which monitor the financial dealing of independent ministries. One of the most prominent of these organizations is the Evangelical Council for Financial Accountability (ECFA), founded in 1979 at the urging of Billy Graham. The code of the ECFA forbids bait-and-switch fund-raising tactics, requires audited financial statements to be available upon request, and forbids family-dominated boards of directors.

Another prominent accountability organization is the Evangelical Financial Integrity Commission (EFICOM), which specifically oversees broadcast ministries. EFICOM was created largely as a response to the televangelism upheaval of 1987.

In an age of understandable and perhaps even healthy suspicion of large broadcast ministries, it is troublesome, if not alarming, that many such ministries do not belong to accountability organizations. Furthermore, there have been virtually no consequences attached to those groups which lose approval of the ECFA or EFICOM, nor has there been any significant public demand for Christian ministries to join accountability organizations. Although not belonging to such an organization is not per se an admission of financial wrongdoing (nor is membership a guarantee of fiscal integrity), in an age of scandal a dark cloud of suspicion looms over nonmember organizations.

It is unfortunate that it took scandals to force many ministries and their supporters into the awareness of the need for financial accountability. Most national ministries, such as "Through the Bible Radio," "The Billy Graham Evangelistic Organization," "World Vision," and "Focus on the Family" have always had impeccable reputations for financial honesty, integrity, and accountability. These groups did not employ sound practices because of pressure but because it was the right thing to do. If organizations refuse to open their books, account for the life-styles of their leaders, or shun membership in accountability organizations, such groups have not earned the right to be financially supported. By law, every nonprofit, 501 (c) (3) organization is required to make available for public inspection on its premises 1) a copy of its annual tax returns on Form 990 for the current year and each of the two preceding years, 2) a copy of its application for tax exemption on Form 1023, and 3) a copy of any correspondence with the IRS regarding tax returns or applications. If a ministry cannot reasonably demonstrate financial accountability, why not choose instead to support ones which can?

2. *Are the ministry leaders morally accountable?*

The harshest words in the Bible are not directed toward unbelievers but toward religious hypocrites. The religious leaders at the time of Christ typically acted pious in public, making sure their "good works" were known to all. Inwardly, however, they were worse than the "common people" they condemned. Hypocrisy among religious leaders is nothing new, and there are biblical checks and balances which protect against such inconsistencies among Christian leaders. Paul the apostle laid down specific requirements for church leaders:

> It is a trustworthy statement: if any man aspires to the office of overseer, it is a fine work he desires to do. An overseer, then, must be above reproach, the husband of one wife, temperate, prudent, respectable, hospitable, able to teach, not addicted to wine or pugnacious, but gentle, uncontentious, free from the love of money. He must be one who manages his own household well, keeping his children under control with all dignity (but if a man does not know how to manage his own household, how will he take care of the church of God?); and not a new convert, lest he become conceited and fall into

the condemnation incurred by the devil. And he must have a good reputation with those outside the church, so that he may not fall into reproach and the snare of the devil (1 Timothy 3:1-7).

These requirements should be used to determine a person's qualifications for leadership before the person is placed in a responsible position. Furthermore, the privilege of being a minister of the gospel carries with it the responsibility of a life consistent with biblical morality. If a leader is involved in moral failure, it is necessary for both the person and the ministry to deal with the root causes. When warranted by the situation, there should be a time for healing and rehabilitation. In extreme cases, the credibility and reputation may never return, demanding a permanent disqualification from the ministry.

Christian leaders, despite the notion that they enjoy comfortable positions, are under tremendous pressure. Besides having lives under constant moral scrutiny, there is also the awesome responsibility of the spiritual well-being of their parishioners. As a result, there is a high degree of "burn out" in the ministry, often due to the immense expectations heaped upon ministers.

Leaders of ministries ought to be encouraged, appreciated, and protected from the temptations which threaten to undermine their work. But Christian leaders are only human and, despite the best intentions, can suffer moral lapse. However, the end does not justify the means. Regardless of a minister's ability to help or "bless" people, if a minister's personal life is in shambles, he has no place in the ministry until the problems are resolved. Practicing forgiveness and restoration to Christian fellowship is important, but a return to the responsibility of church leadership after moral failure is a separate consideration. This is a matter that should be handled by the church in accordance with Scripture, instead of through a popularity poll.

Moral uprightness and accountability are biblical requirements of church leaders, and settling for anything less is a
compromise inconsistent with biblical teachings (Acts 6:3).

3. *Is the ministry accountable for its teaching?*

An often overlooked cause of corruption in religion is
corrupt teaching. The tenets of a belief system usually
determine the values and practices of its followers. When
religious tenets deviate from the orthodox position, whether
intentionally or otherwise, the potential for problems in
faith and practice greatly increases. Too often the leaders of
ministries have little, if any, biblical or theological training.
This frequently causes a doctrinal imbalance, which further creates and perpetuates corrupt and sometimes danger-
ous practices. Paul the apostle warned the church at Rome
about those who teach things contrary to the New Testament: "Now I urge you, brethren, keep your eye on those
who cause dissensions and hindrances contrary to the
teaching which you learned, and turn away from them"
(Romans 16:17).

A recent illustration of the need for doctrinal accountability among ministries is the PTL saga. When the affluent
life-style and moral inconsistencies of Jim Bakker are
examined, one might wonder how he was able to justify his
actions in light of biblical teaching. The answer comes from
understanding one of Bakker's basic assumptions, which is
derived from a doctrine first enunciated in the 1930s. The
basic assumption is that God wants everyone wealthy and
that financial prosperity is a sign of divine blessing.

The man who formulated the doctrine which underlies
the assumption of wealth being a believer's divine right was
E. W. Kenyon. His teaching has become known as the
"prosperity" doctrine, "faith doctrine," "positive confes-
sion," or the "health-and-wealth gospel." The modern
proponents of the viewpoint include evangelists Oral
Roberts, Kenneth Copeland, and Kenneth Hagin. The basic
teaching of the "prosperity" message is taken from Mark

11:24: "Therefore I say to you, all things for which you pray and ask, believe that you have received them, and they shall be granted you."

Those who teach this doctrine emphasize that the key to receiving things is not only asking God but also believing you *have received them*. The believer is to "claim" that the request was granted and "confess" that God has done as was requested. God is considered to be obliged to deliver as demanded.

The first assumption of the prosperity gospel is that God wants everybody well. If someone remains sick, it is considered to be due to sin or lack of faith in the person's life. Health is considered a guaranteed by-product of salvation as long as the believer knows the right formula. The adherents of the prosperity gospel thus place a heavy emphasis on "faith healing." Unfortunately, since the believers are told that they are guaranteed health as long as they have enough faith, those who remain sick are left in a dilemma: Either they pretend they are healed—a response which is the same as what the Christian Science cult teaches—or else they feel condemned for not receiving what they are told God has provided for them.

In the first case, people have thrown away medicine necessary for the survival of themselves and their children, often resulting in a tragic, preventable death. Others have been humiliated when they realize that they have been living in a make-believe world. In the second case, many have been overcome by guilt and despair, blaming themselves for not obtaining divine favor.

The second assumption of the prosperity teaching is that God wants everyone wealthy. Traditional Pentecostals shunned the pleasures of the world. Then along came people like the Bakkers and Oral Roberts who say, "God wants you to be rich and enjoy the pleasures you thought were wrong." Jim Bakker once said, "If you pray for a camper, be sure to tell God what color." At least the Bakkers were consistent in this area. They extracted millions of dollars from the PTL organization and indulged in expensive homes, luxury cars, and extravagant life-styles. This was in line with their assumptions that "God wants us wealthy."

The Bakkers subordinated financial integrity and biblical principles of moderation to the lure of the prosperity doctrine. It was most convenient for them to have not only a common desire to be affluent but a doctrine to support it. Given the millions of dollars available from PTL contributors, the combination led to disaster. The apostle Paul warned Timothy that there will be a time when false teachings will abound:

> For the time will come when they will not endure sound doctrine; but wanting to have their ears tickled, they will accumulate for themselves teachers in accordance to their own desires; and will turn away their ears from the truth, and will turn aside to myths (2 Timothy 4:3,4).

The gospel of health-and-wealth as held by the Bakkers and others is flawed at its very foundation for the Bible does not teach that we create our own reality by "believing" or "confessing." Instead, God is the creator of reality. Prayer is not a means of demanding from God but rather of requesting from God: "If we ask anything *according to His will*, He hears us" (1 John 5:14).

Before supporting a ministry which makes unusual or unorthodox claims, its teachings ought to be examined in light of the Bible. There are many aberrant doctrines being presented today, and lack of discernment on the part of viewers and listeners has led many people into cults. The Bible says not to believe every claim but to test them to see if they are in accordance with what God has revealed (1 John 4:1). Furthermore, Scripture admonishes to "examine everything carefully; hold fast to that which is good." (1 Thessalonians 5:21).

Many who followed the Bakkers' progression into the prosperity gospel with its promise of health and wealth also anticipated that it would eventually take its toll upon them. The seduction of prosperity led Tammy Bakker from a simple life-style, in which wearing makeup was a sin, to extravagance. When Jesus said, "You will know them by their fruits" (Matthew 7:16), He was referring not only to life-style but to doctrine. When a particular teaching produces an immodest or immoral life-style, it should be denounced in the strongest terms.

4. *Is the ministry accountable for its balance?*

The mission of the church—as presented in the New Testament—is evangelism and discipleship. "Evangelism" means simply to present the good news that Jesus died for the sins of the world, and that He offers forgiveness to all who trust in Him. "Discipleship" is teaching believers how to live in accordance with the will of God as revealed in the Bible. There is nothing complicated about the basic mission of the Christian ministry. However, certain television ministries have arisen which have caused confusion about the church's function.

There are "Christian" television programs which are more soap opera than ministry, more entertainment than evangelism. The desire for entertainment is not bad per se, but a steady diet of entertainment under the guise of ministry leads to an imbalanced, unhealthy view of what ministries are supposed to do. The apostle Paul told the church at Ephesus that church leaders are called to prepare God's people for works of service (Ephesians 4:12). This comes first and foremost through serious Bible study. The psalmist said the Word of God "is a lamp to my feet, and a light to my path" (Psalm 119:105). For a balanced faith and spiritual direction the principles of the Bible are to be learned and obeyed.

A ministry's balance can often be determined by the way in which the Bible is utilized. Is Scripture used to strengthen the personal, family, and relational life of the believer, or is it used to manipulate and coerce people to give more money to the "ministry."

Another reason some ministries are imbalanced is that many preachers and evangelists do not have any solid biblical training. It is no wonder that these often succumb to unorthodox, aberrational, or even cultic doctrine since they lack the necessary instruction to sufficiently detect erroneous teachings. The apostle Paul indicated that once a person reaches a mature level of biblical understanding, then a protection from deception exists: "As a result, we are no longer to be children, tossed here and there by waves, and carried about by every wind of doctrine, by the trickery of men, by craftiness in deceitful scheming" (Ephesians 4:14).

When a Christian leader does not have sufficient biblical and theological training, it is imperative that the leader have constant access to reputable, Bible-believing scholars. This practice would help ensure balance and stability.

Leading the Way Out of the Chaos

Change within our culture happens when people work together to confront the problems which exist. Although God has raised up churches and ministries as vehicles to reach the world, it must be remembered that the work of the ministry is done by *all* believers. The role of the church and of legitimate Christian organizations is to equip the saints so that *we* can do the work of the ministry (Ephesians 4:12). In particular, Christian leaders have been called to perform this task of equipping believers for service (Ephesians 4:11). Thus, it is time for us to seek out those churches, ministries, and leaders who, through balanced leadership, are fulfilling their call to equip the saints. The high standards demanded of Christian leaders must be followed (1 Timothy 3:1-7), with a particular emphasis on integrity and accountability. Since God has entrusted His children to leaders who "keep watch over [our] souls" (Hebrews 13:17), there must be wisdom in selecting and supporting these leaders. If problems arise or even appear to arise among those responsible for equipping Christians, we must be discerning, confrontive, and demanding in our quest for solutions. Individually and collectively there are opportunities for us to lead our culture out of the chaos. As we seek to fulfill our own calling to ministry, let us pray the Lord of harvest will send out workers into His harvest (Matthew 9:38).

13

Emerging from the Chaos

Southern California summers can be unbearably hot, and thousands of people seek relief at the beach. The descent from the hot sand to the cool water of the Pacific Ocean brings one face-to-face with the formidable California surf. First-timers who challenge the waves are likely to experience saltwater up the nose and sand in the swimsuit before figuring out how to survive amid the breakers.

I vividly recall one occasion on which I learned the hard way about the awesome power of the ocean. While out in the surf, a large wave began to break at least 50 feet in front of me, as the glassy curl of the wave became a boiling cascade of whitewater. I wasn't out far enough to ride the wave properly and had to quickly decide what course of action to take. Most people who are "caught inside" as I was make the intelligent choice of diving under the wave, which calls for momentarily holding your breath until you emerge in the calm trough behind the wave. I, however, tried to stay upright and keep my head above the oncoming wave. Bad move.

My first recollection was that no matter how high I tried to raise my head, the wave was still higher. With the roar of a locomotive, the turbulent, boiling foam enveloped me, knocking me backward toward the beach. The bright, sunny day disappeared as the wave pounded me down under the water. I recall seeing air bubbles under the bluish-green water, but I still wasn't sure which way was up. After what seemed like an eternity, my roller-coaster ride ended as quickly as it began, with the wave spitting me up on the beach before its power dissipated. Land never felt so wonderful beneath my feet!

That experience at the beach was a microcosm of the turbulent chaos which has enveloped our age. Like the pounding surf, powerful waves of antireligious secularism, rejecting the traditional values so dear to most of us, have swamped our culture. We feel caught in the midst of this confusing, boiling cauldron of new ideas and values. How do we respond? Will we even survive? While some have chosen to panic and others fight to keep their heads above water, God has given us the means to not only survive, but flourish. We can emerge from the chaos and escape from the sea of uncertainty. The enemy which held us under can be identified, understood, and overcome. But the question of whether we will be violently battered again or whether we will emerge victorious depends upon our response: Are we willing, available, and prepared to actively pursue God's way out of the chaos?

Willing, Available, and Prepared

Do we want to emerge from the chaos and discover the abundant life God has for us individually? Do we desire for Christianity to be reestablished as the dominant worldview of our day? The forces of secularism which hold us back from achieving our goals can be overcome *if* we are willing to make the necessary adjustments in the ways we think, believe, and act. But our willingness to succeed must be accompanied by a change of attitude which expects us to succeed. Our sights must not be set so low that we speak of merely surviving amid the chaos. Instead, we need to engage that attitude of winners and employ as our target notions of victory, overcoming, and reemerging. The Bible says we are more than conquerors through Jesus Christ (Romans 8:37), and that He who is in us is greater than he who is in the world (1 John 4:4). Our willingness to rise to the occasion, take charge, and win the battle will largely determine what kind of victory we do in fact achieve.

Willingness is important, but without availability it is a mere pipe dream. Are we available to pursue the battle for our culture? This is not a time to say, "I gave at the office." Too often the concept of "stewardship" is understood to refer to how we use our money. But has not God also made us stewards of our time? He has entrusted us with the responsibility of wisely using our time and efforts. Unless we make ourselves available to carry out the divine plan for the redemption of our civilization, the battle will never be fought and the victory never realized. Even if we gave all of our money to the cause but failed to get directly involved, the battle would not be won. To illustrate the point, suppose instead of spending $100 billion to win the Persian Gulf War, the allies decided to offer $100 billion to the 500,000 Iraqi soldiers (which equates to $200,000 per soldier), provided they left Kuwait? Would this have won the war? The answer is obvious. Wars are not won by merely throwing money at the problem. The price of victory was the commitment of hundreds of thousands of allied troops from several nations who put their lives on the line in order to win. A significant victory and the change which occurs with it is possible only when enough people make themselves available to pursue the objective. Are you available to fight the battle against secularism so that our culture can emerge from the chaos?

The good news is that Christians have a track record of being willing to serve the Lord and even being available for fighting His battles. The bad news, unfortunately, is that willingness and availability fall short of what is needed to reach a lost, chaotic, confused, and secular age. Something is lacking. This missing element is *preparation*. To engage in battle—whether physical, ideological, or spiritual—without proper preparation is virtual suicide, regardless of how willing and available the combatant. The Bible underscores this by warning against the danger of having a zeal for God but not in accordance with knowledge (Romans 10:2). A large segment of Christianity keeps getting clobbered because it has not taken the time to study, analyze, and understand the identity of the enemy and the battle plan mapped out in the Bible. We zealously react to the damage done by the enemy of secularism but fail to recognize the root cause of the damage. This fragmented view has Christians attacking the symptoms instead of the source of the problems. The source of the evils of our day is essentially a shift in worldviews in which reliance on God has been replaced with reliance on man. The abandonment of God in favor of a deified view of man is the "big picture" from which our present cultural chaos flows. Failure to see this "big picture" is what prevents us from effectively combating the social ills we face. As the late Francis Schaeffer wrote, Christians

> ... have very gradually become disturbed over permissiveness, pornography, the public schools, the breakdown of the family, and finally abortion. But they have not seen this as a totality—each thing being a part, a symptom of a larger problem. They have failed to see that all this has come about due to a shift in the world view—that is, through a fundamental change in the way people think and view the world and life as a whole. This shift has been *away from* a world view that was at least vaguely Christian in people's memories ... *toward* something completely different—toward a world view based upon the idea

that the final reality is impersonal matter or energy shaped into its present form by impersonal chance.[1]

Understanding the "big picture" is a vital part of the preparation needed to enable us to emerge from the chaos. Why is it that we have failed to see the chaos of our age as a symptom of a larger problem? Generally because we have failed to be "watchmen on the walls" and have failed to do our homework. Zeal is a poor substitute for understanding the problems of our day, the biblical solutions, and the means to apply these answers in a secular age.

One popular southern California radio commentator, a religious Jew, laments that "evangelicals don't read." He is quite correct. Christians have a tendency to read only friendly material written by fellow travelers in the faith. Books written by secularists, which betray their worldview and the assumptions of the secular mind, are typically avoided. How can the weaknesses of secularism be exploited if they can't even be located, much less understood? If we truly know our enemy, realizing that the cause of many of our social ills is the philosophy of secularism, then we can go beyond fighting the symptoms and strike at the heart of the problem. This knowledge will only come by reading a broad spectrum of books, having dialogue with those who embrace secular thinking, and developing coherent, biblically based answers to the problems of our day. Along with prayer and love, a well-reasoned argument completes the technique used by the early Christians to turn their world upside down. It is our task to prepare for similar encounters and expect similar results.

Scared? Who, Me?

Why should anyone want to leave the warmth of the fireside and the camaraderie of like-minded people to venture into a cold, hostile environment for the purpose of doing battle? Perhaps out of feeblemindedness or some misguided notion of glory and bravado. But there are legitimate reasons for exchanging comfort for confrontation. Just like the soldiers in wartime, we have causes worth living for and dying for. Someone once remarked that it's easy to get people to give their last drop of blood for a cause, but it's more difficult to get them to give their first drop. Martyrs are more plentiful than those who are willing to get their feet wet and be inconvenienced for the cause. Why would someone want to forgo a safe haven of rest for the battlefield? Love and duty stand out as the most prominent of reasons—love for those trapped in the netherworld of chaos and confusion and a sense of duty which compels a person to act in accordance with what he believes to be the will of God. Love and duty are the dynamic means of motivating people to reach beyond themselves, to pursue the redemption of those who will otherwise perish. These are the lives which can be transformed through confrontation with the truth and who, collectively, represent a culture which can be redeemed.

It's natural to be more comfortable with fellow believers than with unbelievers. Furthermore, confronting secularists leaves us vulnerable to rejection. With fragile self-esteem and the typical shortfall of confidence serving as barriers to confronting unbelievers on their own ideological turf, it's far easier to avoid engaging the opposition. But despite these seemingly good reasons for keeping to ourselves, all the obstacles to challenging secularism can be overcome.

I have sensed the discomfort many of the listeners to my radio show experience when I have notorious unbelievers, skeptics, and opponents of biblical morality as guests. Yet I continue to attempt to bring a balanced diet of controversial people and issues to my audience because I'm committed to providing them with what I feel they *need* to hear instead of what they *want* to hear. What has been the result? The audience has heard me take the time to hear out the secularists, appreciate their position, and understand what it is they truly believe. Usually there is also common ground discovered between their position and mine. All this gives me the chance to express my concern for them as people, to love them despite their beliefs, and to contrast their views with that of the Bible. Furthermore, their faulty assumptions and the inconsistencies of their view often become readily. apparent for the audience to see. Finally, these encounters give the opportunity to clear up for my secularist guests the misconceptions they tend to have about Christianity. Some of them labor under the weirdest and most bizarre impressions of what Christianity teaches, primarily due to the fact that no one has taken the time to explain what we truly believe. When these matters are resolved, I've seen many people take a renewed interest in finding out what Christianity offers.

My approach to secularists and other types of unbelievers on the radio is in part designed to be a model for how we can deal intelligently, lovingly, and productively with those of differing views. I encourage those who are willing, available, and prepared to confront such people to not be discouraged by less than dramatic results. While we may not be successful in our first attempts at engaging the secularist, practice and perseverance will eventually reap tremendous dividends in the battle for our culture. Remember the unwritten beatitude: "Blessed are the flexible, for they shall not be broken." Our resilience, even in the face of rejection, is further evidence that the gospel is here to stay.

Destiny in Our Hands

I was chatting with a studio makeup artist once and heard from him a fascinating story. In 1960 he was chosen to provide the makeup for Vice President Richard Nixon, who was running for the presidency against a young Massachusetts senator, John F. Kennedy. Nixon and Kennedy were scheduled to participate in the first of three nationally televised presidential debates.

The makeup artist knew from experience that Nixon's beard was heavy and that the bright television lights would pick up his "five-o-clock shadow" unless makeup was properly applied. Unfortunately, Nixon arrived late. When the makeup man stepped out to hastily apply the makeup, he was brushed aside by Nixon's wife. As the makeup man stood holding the unused tools of his trade, Mrs. Nixon applied some of her own translucent makeup before the Vice President rushed onstage.

After the debate, political analysts surveyed numerous people for their reactions, and the results were most startling. The majority of the radio audience felt that Nixon had won the debate. Those who watched the event on television primarily thought Kennedy had prevailed. How can this discrepancy be explained? The radio audience based its judgment on the quality of the presentation, while many in the television audience claimed that the contrasting appearance between Nixon and Kennedy was the deciding factor. Kennedy appeared robust and healthy, while Nixon looked haggard and sickly, due primarily to the glare of the television lights shining off his translucent makeup.

In one of the closest presidential elections of all time, Kennedy defeated Nixon and became the thirty-fifth president of the United States. A few more votes for Nixon in key states would have changed the outcome. Some analysts and historians have determined that the first Nixon-Kennedy debate gave Kennedy the margin of victory. Had Nixon looked better, he might have swayed the television audience the way he did the radio audience. The difference was the makeup. That makeup artist held in his hands the key to the presidency of the United States and, perhaps, the future of the world. What might have happened if he had been able to use the tools of his trade? We will never know for certain because what he held in his hands was not put to use.

Those who know Jesus Christ as personal Lord and Savior have tools, also. God's plan for this world as found in the Scriptures has been entrusted to us. It is the means for bringing order from chaos. We possess a message which has the ability to transform the lives of individuals, as well as society as a whole. The biblical plan enables us to emerge from the chaos and reestablish the dominance of Christian values in the areas of law, media, ethics, the family, government, and education. It's too late to change the outcome of the 1960 presidential election where the tools were not used. But it isn't too late for us to use what God has placed in our hands to shape the destiny of civilization. The question is, This time will we use the tools we hold in our hands?

NOTES

Chapter 4—The Turmoil over Ethics and Morality

1. James R. Adair, *Saints Alive* (Van Kampen Press, 1951), p. 149.
2. Adair, pp. 154-55.
3. Adair, p. 155.

Chapter 5—The Decline of Education

1. Kenneth O. Gangel, citing a report of the statement by Paul Kienel, "How Will our Family Benefit?" H. Wayne House, ed., *Schooling Choices* (Multnomah Press, 1988), p. 131.
2. Christina Hoff Summers, "Ethics Without Virtue: Moral Education in America," *American Scholar*, Summer 1984, p. 381.
3. Gangel, pp. 126-27.
4. Ronald Nash, *The Closing of the American Heart* (Probe Books, 1990), p. 56.
5. Quoted by Susan Rose, *Keeping Them Out of the Hands of Satan: Evangelical Schooling in America* (Routledge, 1989), p. 39.
6. Richard M. Weaver, *Visions of Order* (Louisiana State University Press, 1964), p. 115.
7. Samuel L. Blumenfeld, *Is Public Education Necessary?* (Devin-Adair, 1981), p. 5.
8. Reginald G. Damerell, *Education's Smoking Gun: How Teachers' Colleges Have Destroyed Education in America* (Fruendlich, 1985), p. 13.
9. Blumenfeld, *NEA: Trojan Horse in American Education* (The Paradigm Co., 1984), p. 211.

Chapter 7—A Brave New Secular Future

1. Quoted by Francis Schaeffer and C. Everett Koop, *Whatever Happened to the Human Race?* (Revell, 1979), p. 73.
2. Quoted by Schaeffer and Koop, *Whatever Happened*, p. 73.
3. *Los Angeles Times*, September 26, 1988, Metro, p. 3.
4. *Washington Post*, February 29, 1976.
5. *Orange County Register*, (Santa Ana, CA), January 22, 1988, A1.

Chapter 8—The Abandonment of Media

1. Dinesh O'Souza, "TV News: The Politics of Social Climbing," *Human Events*, August 16, 1986, p. 12.
2. *Newsweek*, April 24, 1989.
3. *Washington Post*, March 25, 1990.
4. *Los Angeles Times*, July 1, 1990.
5. Nikos Kazantzakis, *Saviors of God* (Simon & Schuster, 1969).

Chapter 10—The Polarizing Effect of the Pro-Life Movement
1. English translation of the text of the decision by Robert E. Jonas and John D. Gorby, "West German Abortion Decision: A Contrast to *Roe v Wade*–with Commentaries," 9 John Marshall Journal of Practice and Procedure, 1976, p. 638.
2. John Bartlett, *Bartlett's Familiar Quotations*, 15th ed., (Little, Brown and Company, 1980), p. 824.

Chapter 13—Emerging from the Chaos
1. Francis A. Schaeffer, *A Christian Manifesto* (Crossway Books, 1981), pp. 17-18.

Dear Reader:

We would appreciate hearing from you regarding this Harvest House nonfiction book. It will enable us to continue to give you the best in Christian publishing.

1. What most influenced you to purchase *God in the Chaos*?
   - ☐ Author
   - ☐ Subject matter
   - ☐ Backcover copy
   - ☐ Recommendations
   - ☐ Cover/Title
   - ☐ _____

2. Where did you purchase this book?
   - ☐ Christian bookstore
   - ☐ General bookstore
   - ☐ Department store
   - ☐ Grocery store
   - ☐ Other

3. Your overall rating of this book:
   - ☐ Excellent ☐ Very good ☐ Good ☐ Fair ☐ Poor

4. How likely would you be to purchase other books by this author?
   - ☐ Very likely
   - ☐ Somewhat likely
   - ☐ Not very likely
   - ☐ Not at all

5. What types of books most interest you?
   (check all that apply)
   - ☐ Women's Books
   - ☐ Marriage Books
   - ☐ Current Issues
   - ☐ Self Help/Psychology
   - ☐ Bible Studies
   - ☐ Fiction
   - ☐ Biographies
   - ☐ Children's Books
   - ☐ Youth Books
   - ☐ Other _____

6. Please check the box next to your age group.
   - ☐ Under 18
   - ☐ 18-24
   - ☐ 25-34
   - ☐ 35-44
   - ☐ 45-54
   - ☐ 55 and over

Mail to: Editorial Director
Harvest House Publishers
1075 Arrowsmith
Eugene, OR 97402

Name _____

Address _____

City _____ State _____ Zip _____

**Thank you for helping us to help you
in future publications!**